THE HARMS OF BEAUTY

Studies in Social Harm

Series editors: **Christina Pantazis**, *University of Bristol* *and* **Simon Pemberton**, *University of Birmingham*

The Studies in Social Harms series seeks to understand the production of harm within contemporary society. The series offers comparative and international perspectives to understand the distribution of harm and combines new theory and empirical research.

Also available in the series:

Border Harms and Everyday Violence
Evgenia Iliadou

Against Youth Violence
Luke Billingham and **Keir Irwin-Rogers**

The Harms of Work
Anthony Lloyd

Labour Exploitation and Work-Based Harm
Sam Scott

Harmful Societies
Simon A. Pemberton

Find out more at:
bristoluniversitypress.co.uk/studies-in-social-harm

THE HARMS OF BEAUTY

Sam Barnes

With a Foreword by
Georgios A. Antonopoulos

BRISTOL
UNIVERSITY
PRESS

First published in Great Britain in 2025 by

Bristol University Press
University of Bristol
1–9 Old Park Hill
Bristol
BS2 8BB
UK
t: +44 (0)117 374 6645
e: bup-info@bristol.ac.uk

Details of international sales and distribution partners are available at bristoluniversitypress.co.uk

British Library Cataloguing in Publication Data
A catalogue record for this book is available from the British Library

ISBN 978-1-5292-3533-3 hardcover
ISBN 978-1-5292-3535-7 ePub
ISBN 978-1-5292-3536-4 ePdf

Cover design: Bristol University Press
Front cover image: 123rf/erstudiostok
Bristol University Press uses environmentally responsible print partners.
Printed and bound in Great Britain by CPI Group (UK) Ltd, Croydon, CR0 4YY

FSC
www.fsc.org
MIX
Paper | Supporting responsible forestry
FSC® C013604

Contents

Series Editors' Preface

We are very pleased to publish the seventh book in the *Studies in Social Harm* series. Our series, which began in 2014, aims to provide novel and cutting edge analysis of the serious harms that affect society. Transversing disciplinary boundaries, the series aims to highlight some of the most damaging harms which evade legal sanction and often public scrutiny too. These harms affect human and non-human species and increasingly the planet and environment. Employing different theoretical perspectives and methodological approaches and novel investigations, the book series addresses key questions relating to what harms, how, and why. Ultimately, it is through the posing of these questions that we can address how harms can be mitigated.

Sam Barnes' *Harms of Beauty* presents a fascinating account of the wide ranging harms associated with the burgeoning beauty industry. Seeking to move away from an approach which labels young people as deviant, Barnes' investigation involves a rich ethnography to better understand young people pursuit of beauty. Although the desire for beauty has been ever present, Barnes' book explores how this obsession with beauty in capitalist societies has become associated with hyper-individualised competitive consumer culture fuelled by the rapid proliferation of legal, illegal and counterfeit beauty markets. Barnes' definition of beauty products and services is broad, encompassing "skincare, haircare, and make-up products, cosmetic injectables, perfume and aftershaves, weight-loss drugs, teeth whitening products and procedures, and anti-ageing and tanning products … fitness and healthy eating regimes … so-called 'health and wellbeing' products", as well plastic surgery and health tourism. Whilst traditionally criminological analyses have tended to focus on the [physical] harms of illicit products, Barnes encourages readers to see connections between illicit and licit beauty markets, making a compelling argument for understanding beauty harms as embedded within the political economy of consumer capitalism which encourages empowerment through beauty enhancement. Through this perspective, beauty harms are often culturally accepted and normalised in everyday life rather than seen as an aberration. Through Barnes' ethnographic study of sellers and consumers, we learn about the destructive nature of beauty in the lives of young people in England. In doing so, Barnes provides us with a theoretically and empirically compelling critique of contemporary consumer culture which is harming not only individuals but also the planet.

Christina Pantazis
Simon Pemberton

Acknowledgements

I would like to take this opportunity to thank a number of professional colleagues who have provided some invaluable feedback and support for this book. As this book is based upon my PhD studies, I would first like to thank my PhD supervision team – Georgios Antonopoulos, Louise Wattis and Jo Large. My thanks also go to other academics who have helped shape the book's arguments and provided support, advice and discussions over the years including Professor Daniel Briggs, Dr Mark Bushell, Professor James Treadwell, Dr Tammy Ayres and Dr Alex Hall. A special thank you is owed to Dr Robert Lee. Rob generously read through numerous drafts, provided remarkably helpful comments to shape this book and challenged me intellectually to produce work that I am truly proud of.

A big thank you must go to everyone who took part in the research and allowed me to enter into your world. I appreciate the time you dedicated to talking with me. I would also like to express my gratitude to Bristol University Press and the Studies in Social Harm series for believing in the book and giving this work a home. Finally, I owe everything to my mum and dad. Without their endless love and support I would not be writing this.

Foreword

Georgios A. Antonopoulos
Professor of Criminology,
Northumbria University

The (Looking) 'Good', the 'Bad' and the 'Ugly'

It is a great pleasure being given the opportunity to introduce Sam Barnes' first book to readers. As one of Barnes' supervisors of her PhD thesis, which this book is based upon, I was able to personally witness her systematic approach, hard work and resourcefulness in the field, which the end-product is a testament to. *The Harms of Beauty* is an original work, which fully does what it promises: 'it explores the wide array of harms associated with legal, illegal and counterfeit markets within the beauty industry to develop an understanding of supply and demand beyond a traditional criminological framework'. Written with the crispness that is the result of state-of-the-art knowledge, this impeccably organized book is based on eight chapters that seamlessly link to one another, covering both the demand and the supply side of an industry with an overlooked sinister side.

Drawing upon advances in ultra-realism, zemiology and deviant leisure (see Hall and Winlow, 2015; Raymen and Smith, 2019), Barnes theorizes on the changing nature of identity, leisure and consumption in late capitalism (see also Hall, 2019). The work is based on a remarkable methodological effort: an ethnographic, 'offline' study in a town in the southeast of England, which Barnes refers to as 'Beaufort', as well as observations and interviews carried out in relevant settings in East London, neighbouring towns to 'Beaufort' and in online spaces.

Barnes offers an extremely rich account on the changing nature of beauty and fashion, and shows how within this context, harmful practices are not only accepted but also widely celebrated. Barnes' historical insights in the first part of the book show that harmful practices and associated risks have always been inherent to the pursuit and consumption of beauty and have been normalized. However, what is different about late capitalism is the scale and diffusion of these harmful practices, facilitated by globalization, the hegemony of consumer culture, privatized healthcare and beauty regimes, as well as the proliferation of information and communication technologies that have created a hyper-connectedness shaping to a great extent the demand and supply of beauty consumption.

Barnes explores beauty product sellers' varied motivations and drivers for their business as well as the way in which they manage risks associated with the business. The author very skilfully presents and contextualizes the ways in which the forces of neoliberalism have created an environment in which actors in the business oscillate between entrepreneurship and consumption. Many of these actors understand how important it is for one to be 'beautiful' in modern society, so not only do they make a bit of money but also become brokers of beauty at the 'gym' and at the 'salon'. Unsurprisingly, the archetypical 'bad' in representations of illegal markets, the 'organized criminals', are not present among Barnes' protagonists.

The author deals with beauty as capital in contemporary society and economy, explores how 'looking good' allows one to retain an element of control over one's life, and becomes an asset that contributes towards the improvement of one's social and working life. Barnes also focuses on how social media change expectations of the 'normal', shape subjective experiences, expose (young) people to unrealistic images of beauty and to appearance ideals that are not attainable (or sustainable), and which, via endless comparisons, result in beauty consumption practices and patterns that carry significant risks. Finally, Barnes offers a unique account of 'Botox parties' and how consuming beauty together and participating in beauty rituals were essential for a female friendship group of beauty consumers, the 'Clique'.

Barnes handles incredibly lively and engaging data from a variety of actors, including those who engage in sometimes parasuicidal activities in society, which is, in Barnes' words, 'marked by hyper-comparison, hyper-consumption and competitive individualism'. Unlike the harms of the beauty industry being presented as a product of 'deviance' of one type or another, the author very skilfully weaves accounts on the wider social, cultural, economic as well as technological developments, showing that those developments' 'resultant force' is hyper-conformity with the values and soul of the neoliberal consumer culture.

Needless to say, this rudimentary presentation of some of the main discussion points in the book does not do justice to their richness or the amount of work that has been put into the process. This is a very interesting piece of work, and I am confident that readers will share my enthusiasm about it. Most impressive is the text's balance on various terrains. This book is a remarkable amalgamate of serious and vivid empirical research and theoretical prowess, nuanced criminological/sociological analysis with an accessible, grounded writing style, and also a fast-paced, gripping account that is filled with insight and calm evaluations. In my opinion, those who read it will find their ideas stretched. Barnes' book is the epitome of good social science: an entertaining and enlightening read that is essential for anyone trying to figure out what the ugly side of beauty is.

1

Introduction

This book explores the wide array of harms associated with legal, illegal and counterfeit markets within the beauty industry to develop an understanding of supply and demand beyond a traditional criminological framework. Drawing upon data from a detailed ethnographic study, this book examines a small population of beauty-dependent consumers attempting to navigate a society characterized by hyper-comparison, hyper-consumption and competitive individualism. More specifically, it looks at the day-to-day struggles and challenges of young people in contemporary society as they attempt to keep up with the rising beauty standards and expectations of what is considered 'normal'. I write this book to highlight the toxicity of the consumer culture that is driving individuals' willingness to harm themselves, others and the environment in their pursuit of image and body perfection. The latter part of this chapter gives a more comprehensive breakdown of the book's structure, but, for now, I aim to provide insight into the ongoing expansion of the beauty industry and where the idea for this project stemmed from.

The beauty industry

The global beauty industry has seen substantial growth in recent years. In 2023 the personal care and beauty industry contributed a total of £27.2 billion to the UK's economy, an 11 per cent increase from 2022 (British Beauty Council, 2024). From skincare, haircare and make-up products to cosmetic injectables, weight management and fitness products and services, consumers today invest significant time and money to enhance their appearance. The consumption of beauty has extended beyond the everyday use and application of products to include a range of procedures, services and lifestyle choices focused on self-care, nutrition, fitness and overall wellness (Cederström and Spicer, 2015). Alongside the surging popularity of legal beauty products and services, there has been an increase in the usage of lifestyle drugs more generally (Hall, 2019; Gibbs, 2023). At the same time, there has been a significant rise in people undergoing cosmetic surgeries and non-surgical cosmetic procedures in the UK, as well as abroad through the burgeoning interest in medical tourism, whereby individuals travel abroad to have medical, surgical or dental treatments (Holliday et al, 2019) that are deemed inaccessible or prohibitively expensive in their domestic health systems.

Revolutionary developments in information and communication technologies have expanded the sale and consumption of beauty. With the rise of e-commerce platforms, the barriers to accessing and consuming beauty have significantly lowered, and consumers can readily purchase their desired products and services at the click of a button. This accessibility of beauty is seen further through the proliferation of social media and the accompanying rise of beauty influencers and vloggers. These individuals share tutorials and post content promoting their favourite brands to their audiences and, as such, have democratized the discovery and purchasing of new products. Alongside this expansion is the circulation of innumerable resources, providing consumers with guidance on the 'best' way to consume and apply the treatments and products they purchase. In line with this, the increased interest in physical and virtual leisure spaces has intensified the emphasis on appearance and corporeal improvement. To this end, beauty is a significant tool for the contemporary consumer, fulfilling a range of everyday functions. These can include the enhancement of the face; improving the complexion; improving social standing and leisure experiences; increasing the chance of securing a job or further work; and regaining a sense of control over their everyday lives. In a hyper-individualized competitive consumer culture, filled with pressures and insecurities about appearances, work and general life, some young people use quick-fix beauty and healthcare products that promise to make people feel better about themselves and assuage anxieties.

Although the industry is geared towards empowering individuals, there exists a dark and harmful side to beauty that rarely ranks high on the criminological agenda. The production, circulation and consumption of a wide range of unlicensed, counterfeit and 'grey area' beauty products and services generate substantial harm for those involved. It is here that the central motivations for this project can be found. Beginning with an initial encounter with a Facebook advert promoting and selling counterfeit branded beauty products, it quickly became apparent that such products were the tip of the iceberg. Following a thorough search online it became clear that, if consumers were to look in the right places, not only would they be able to purchase counterfeit products, but also services administering both licit and illicit enhancements. Social media is filled with people sharing videos of themselves being injected or injecting others with a range of cosmetic enhancements. While this is not always illicit, it became evident that there was a huge 'grey' market that has, until now, been largely ignored within existing criminological debates.

Background to counterfeiting

While counterfeiting is far from a new phenomenon, with examples going back for hundreds of years (Chaudhry and Zimmerman, 2013), socio-economic and political factors and the evolving nature of technological advances – especially the internet – have all contributed to a widespread and burgeoning trade in counterfeit markets. Counterfeit goods are unauthorized replicas of authentic products, and a vast amount of them now infiltrate physical and virtual spaces. Over the years, interest surrounding counterfeiting as a crime issue has increased. Underpinned by various assumptions that counterfeiting causes economic, societal and consumer harm, official agencies and campaign groups offer extensive arguments for anti-counterfeiting. Yet a quantifiable amount of research has consistently eschewed a distinction between different types of counterfeits when exploring the 'harms' and 'costs' of counterfeiting. For example, the OECD (1998) report on counterfeiting discusses the economic impact of counterfeiting. In doing so, they highlight the harms that emerge from counterfeiting as 'costs', categorizing them in four fundamental ways: costs to the right holder, costs to the countries that are manufacturing the goods, costs to the countries that are retailing and social costs. The OECD (1998) report and the follow-up OECD (2008) report still provide clear and significantly valuable overviews of the fundamental issues facing policy makers and law enforcements agencies in their attempts to combat counterfeiting.

In this vein, most counterfeiting research has centred on the potential risks it poses for public safety and business stability (OECD, 2022), and the alleged connections counterfeiting has with organized crime and terrorism (Naylor, 2002; Home Office, 2022). It seems that the explanations for supplying and consuming counterfeits quickly became a way to pathologize and label groups as 'deviant'.[1] But the reality is that framing counterfeiting as a crime issue can limit the scope of understanding and addressing the problem (Large, 2018). While this is not an attempt to dismiss the more visible harms of the criminal acts that counterfeiting is associated with, the way in which harm has been explored has sidelined the less visible harms that are located within the social structures of late modernity (Pemberton, 2015).

Another observation to make is that research on manifestations of 'organized crime' and illicit markets in the UK is limited and has only recently gained notable attention in criminological research.[2] While there has been an increase in work concerned with counterfeits and their associated harms, little is known about the nature of illicit and counterfeit beauty markets. The existing research on counterfeit markets has identified a range of counterfeit products available, with online and offline markets offering products such as fashion products (Treadwell, 2011; Large, 2019), pharmaceuticals and lifestyle drugs (Lavorgna, 2014; Hall and Antonopoulos, 2016; Gibbs, 2023), alcohol and tobacco (Antonopoulos, 2007; Antonopoulos and Hall, 2015; Shen and Antonopoulos, 2017) and CDs and DVDs (Antonopoulos et al, 2011). However, as we shall see, the counterfeiting of beauty products and their associated harms is very much a burgeoning area that demands greater criminological attention.

Beauty and harm

The beauty industry poses a set of additional challenges for criminology. The focus here is on a broad notion of beauty, which encapsulates a range of products and procedures, for example, skincare, haircare and make-up products, cosmetic injectables, perfume and aftershaves, weight-loss drugs, teeth whitening products and procedures, anti-ageing and tanning products, so-called 'health and wellbeing' products and also fitness and healthy eating regimes. In the context of the relationship between crime and harm, arguments against illicit beauty heavily rely on notions of physical harm associated the use of beauty products and services and are often grounded in a public health perspective (see Intellectual Property, 2024). Here, emphasis is placed on the possible dangers consumers face following poorly performed cosmetic enhancements and the consumption of pharmaceuticals when self-managing healthcare regimes. Examples include harms arising from products used through poor practice or from inherent risks associated with the administration or application of the product (for example, rashes, swelling, toxicity, fever, headaches, bleeding or reactions to general anaesthesia) (Cook and Dwyer, 2017; Nuffield Council on Bioethics, 2017). However, many of these debates fail to engage with a thorough and critical consideration of the wider social harms accompanying such consumption.

To best understand the consumption of illicit beauty it is necessary to examine it as a component of normal consumer behaviour, and not as something abnormal or outside of standard consumer practices (Large, 2019). It would be simple to assign an understanding of illicit beauty as something that is 'deviant' or transgressive if we were going to ignore the fact that the consumption of illicit goods is fundamentally an extension of the consumption of licit goods (Large, 2018). Consequently, it is deeply problematic to consider it alone and as separate from the licit market. Doing so would indicate a failure to fully engage with and recognize the harms perpetuated by the legitimate beauty industry and how such harms are embedded within the broader political economy of consumer capitalism (Hall et al, 2008; Large, 2018; Raymen and Smith, 2019). It is in this point that one of the central tenets of this book is found. The harms associated with the legal market need to be critically examined with a focus on the overlapping and inextricable relationship of both licit and illicit markets. A fundamental critique of consumer culture is required to consider the harms that are culturally accepted and normalized in the everyday experiences of late capitalism (Hall, 2019). To explore the harms that lie beneath the surface of consumption and supply, a range of theoretical approaches and concepts inform the study, including zemiology, deviant leisure and ultra-realist perspectives. These theoretical approaches are examined in further detail in Chapter 2.

To this end, this book addresses a significant gap in research surrounding the broad range of harms related to the counterfeit and illicit beauty industry and the willingness for individuals to self-harm and inflict harm on others and the environment in the pursuit of self-interest and 'ideal' perfection. Through its examination of the illicit and licit beauty industry, my study resonates with other work within the context of hyper-conformity (Kotzé and Antonopoulos, 2019; Gibbs, 2023). The 'new economy of the self' advertises and offers the late-capitalist subject a continual stream of products and services promising individual enhancement (Hall, 2019: 162). An incessant demand for aesthetic improvement drives the late-capitalist subject towards the expanding range of beauty products and services. From counterfeit make-up to facial injectables and weight-loss drugs, both the use and supply of illicit beauty products and treatments have arguably reached the point of normalization. Whether applying make-up to go to work, injecting cosmetic enhancements in the face or consuming toxic substances to whiten or darken the skin, the consumption of beauty is driven by the desire to address a sense of lack about our appearance that has been cultivated by consumer culture.

As the traditional building blocks of identity, social standing, community ties and relationships have been diminished, a new underlying sense of lack and subsequent desire has evolved. Ultra-realism's analysis of the realities of life assert that crime and deviance are a consequence of the deeper forces, processes and structures of global consumer culture. Beauty use and supply, too, are a product of the deep-rooted systems and pressures inherent in consumer culture. Consuming and supplying licit and illicit beauty products and services are essential for navigating, surviving and succeeding in a society which is marked by hyper-comparison, hyper-consumption and competitive individualism. We become besieged by pervasive feelings of objectless anxiety, insecurity and depression, as our adherence to consumer capitalism leads to a range of socially corrosive and subjective harms. Therefore, to understand beauty use and supply, and the current system of illicit and counterfeit regulation and prohibition, it is fundamental to consider the historical context and development of capitalism.

This book makes a number of important, original contributions to knowledge. Despite some recent attention on the lifestyle drugs trade by Gibbs (2023) and Hall (2019), the broader harms associated with the counterfeit beauty market are often overlooked and ignored. This is the first ethnographic study that attempts to understand the connections between the counterfeit beauty industry and the landscape of late capitalism to explain why young people are more open to not only harming others but also harming themselves. This book intends to avoid the pitfalls of existing perspectives on counterfeiting, which have too far often consistently eschewed a broader understanding of harm, consumption and global capitalism. In doing so, it seeks to move beyond traditional accounts of crime, harm and deviance to better offer a critique of the current landscape of consumer capitalism and its inherent potential for a myriad of individual and social harms to occur (Hall and Winlow, 2015; Raymen and Smith, 2019). By using a harm perspective as a lens through which to view the nature of the beauty industry, this study positively contributes new knowledge to the literature on counterfeit markets and harm. This is done with an attentiveness to the mutating harms of the twenty-first century, which are the root of many of our existential anxieties and societal depression. It reveals how the competitive individualism and hyper-comparison at the heart of contemporary society appears to be the catalyst behind the willingness of the young people in this study to inflict self-harm, harm on others and their environments. In forging strong theoretical links between the beauty industry and the wider economic, technological, social and cultural forces, this book demonstrates how beauty use and supply are hyper-conformist to the underlying values of neoliberal consumer culture and that, arguably, young people are selling counterfeits and consuming beauty as a way to consume the body and consumer lifestyle they want. It is my hope that this study can make a small contribution to an understanding of the dark side of the beauty industry.

Methodological note

The data presented in this book is the product of an ethnographic study that, in part, is a response to the lack of research offering a lived-experience perspective of the ways in which macro-level socio-economic changes and pressures exert themselves on young people. Much of the existing literature in this space often heavily relies on official statistics, consequently ignoring the significant number of harms that are perpetuated by the legitimate industry and embedded within the political economy of consumer capitalism (Hall and Winlow, 2015; Smith and Raymen, 2018; Large, 2018). While such use of statistics serves as a foundation for further discussion, social scientists need to interrogate issues in greater detail to better understand the subject of counterfeiting and gain a 'clear, first-hand picture' (Liebow, 2003: 6) of the relationship between illicit markets and harm. As such, I began by my own investigations using both elements of traditional offline ethnography alongside a contemporary element of virtual ethnography to provide innovative explorations of the underlying motivations, desires and realities of consumers and sellers.

Most of the offline element of fieldwork was carried out in a town in the southeast of England, which I refer to as 'Beaufort'.[3] The research participants for my offline work consisted of 14 young people aged between 18 and 29, the majority of whom lived and worked in or near Beaufort (except for one seller, 'David' who lived and traded in London). Observations and interviews were also carried out in East London, neighbouring towns to Beaufort and in online spaces. I spent a total of 22 months with these people studying what daily life was all about for them; how they found themselves willing to engage in harmful practices of selling, consuming and using licit, illicit and counterfeit beauty; and how they negotiated harm when engaging in these risky activities. From the outset it was clear that their desperate attempt to enhance the 'self' was related to changes in the global economic, technological, social and political landscape, which over time have been internalized and reproduced in a destructive form of illicit beauty use that has compromised their own internal health and wellbeing in favour of an idealized exterior. Young people work, live and socialize in the face of an intense form of hyper-comparison, driving their readiness to do anything they can to be the best or most successful and gain advantages over others, no matter the cost.

Welcome to Beaufort

'Beaufort' is a medium sized town that lacks any level of ethnic diversity and is best described as a commuter town with accessible links to London. I was confident that my experience and knowledge of the history, geography and life of Beaufort would prove invaluable in conducting the fieldwork. Beaufort is a working-class area and has little commercial or industrial activity aside from a small amount of locally-based businesses. Akin to many areas in the UK, Beaufort high-street has seen shops closing at a record rate (see Hooker, 2023). While some shops remain empty, a large number have been transformed into hair, nail, eyebrow and tanning salons. Sustained by leisure and services, alongside beauty and hair salons, much of the high-street consists of pubs and food outlets, while surrounding the high-street are numerous gyms and open spaces including woods, parks and meadows. The town tends to host a variety of community events and the town's nightlife is far from a 24-hour city, with pubs and bars closing at around 1 am.

Immersing myself in the streets of Beaufort as a potential buyer for cheap yet adequate beauty products, I engaged in many conversations with sellers and other potential consumers. Ethnographic data collection involved spending as much time as possible within these communities to achieve an in-depth understanding of the everyday lives of beauty consumers and sellers. However, I could not limit and isolate the study of counterfeiting and beauty from the wider orbits, challenges and desires in participants' lives. I aimed to observe and converse with consumers and sellers in natural, everyday settings and, of course, in addition to shopping, this involved socializing and participating in a range of leisure activities and social events that participants would normally engage it. The interviews and observations for this fieldwork were carried out in a diversity of settings: in shopping centres, at markets, in gyms, at pubs, bars and coffee shops, in respondent's homes and even at 'Botox parties'.[4] An element of covert observation was employed throughout the course of the research to elicit rich data on occasions where I was unfamiliar with the environment, or the people present were merely acquaintances of those I knew. This had the benefit of attaining data I would not have achieved if I had been conducting structured interviews in unfamiliar settings. In doing so, I was able to gain an insight into the role beauty and counterfeiting occupied within the wider struggles and anxieties of their lives.

The online world

The online element involved virtual ethnography to explore the illicit beauty industry in virtual spaces and communities. Contemporary life tends to involve a large amount of time spent in the virtual sphere and virtual communities. This increase of people online has expanded and led to an increase in the number of business-to-business (B2B), business-to-consumer (B2C), and consumer-to-consumer (C2C) marketplaces, platforms and websites (Castells, 2001). The emergence of social networking sites (for example, Facebook) and forms of virtual communication to broad audiences (for example, blogging) indicate how the internet has become embedded in everyday life (Hine, 2015). Such a transformation to the way in which people communicate and consume content necessitated an approach to the research that would generate insights into how such spaces are engaged with.

As a regular user of social networking sites, specifically Facebook and Instagram, I was familiar with how to use these and joined numerous private and public beauty-related Facebook groups. Additionally, I followed a wide variety of beauty brand advocates on Instagram, including celebrities, bloggers and social media influencers[5] promoting products. I began speaking with people in online forums, through social networking sites and marketplaces. Covert observations were utilized during interactions with online sellers and consumers, as well as in situations where I was more interested in the dynamic of a particular online community or space. Conversations occurred over e-mails and private message functions on social media and marketplaces, and I was also able to connect with consumers of beauty and illicit beauty products on Instagram and within Facebook groups related to beauty and fitness. This allowed me to access information about consumption habits and the types of suppliers that consumers used to access products. In addition, through the exchange of Instagram messages, I was able to gain a level of trust with one online seller of beauty counterfeits (Craig) who, it transpired, lived in Beaufort and became one of the offline participants.

Structure of the book

This book is divided into eight chapters which aim to provide an insight into the harms associated with the beauty industry. In Chapter 2 I offer a broad theorization of the changing nature of identity, leisure and consumption in late capitalism, situating the use and supply of beauty products and services within a wider theoretical discussion of subjectivity, socio-economic change, harm and the legitimate beauty industry. I first offer an introduction to the school of ultra-realism (Hall and Winlow, 2015) and its roots in the transcendental materialism theory of subjectivity, before turning my attention to the impact of the pernicious interconnection between the increasingly unstable and fluid job market, the culture of hyper-competitive consumer capitalism and a widespread culture of hyper-consumption and hyper-comparison. Finally, I demonstrate how the harms associated with the illicit beauty industry are closely tied to broader processes of consumerism, emphasizing the need for a critical understanding of global consumer culture and political change. Chapter 3 provides a theorization of the changing nature of beauty, style and fashion, exploring the normalized, accepted and culturally celebrated harmful and harming beauty practices beyond the neoliberal era to contemporary times. Within this, I consider how late modernity has accelerated and amplified the harmful and harming practices and processes related to the use and supply of beauty and fashion.

Chapter 4 moves into the more ethnographic part of this book, which spans Chapters 4 to 7. Chapter 4 operationalizes the earlier theoretical discussions to contextualize the role of supply within the pressures and realities of the participants' lived experiences. This chapter nuances existing arguments by illuminating how supply is operationalized in practice and explores seller motivations in a wider context of the troubles which they face in contemporary society. This discussion pays particular attention to how the powerful forces of neoliberalism have blurred the boundaries between the consumer and supplier, allowing sellers to move flexibly between the two positions in the pursuit of their consumer lifestyle. Chapter 5 builds upon the previous chapter, presenting how consuming and supplying illicit goods and services is both conformist and essential for surviving in the contemporary landscape of consumer capitalism. Offering an insight into beauty consumption and beauty identities, this chapter addresses the role of beauty as capital in contemporary society, exploring how looking good is now considered to improve both social and working lives. Through empirical evidence, it offers an extensive view of the nature of beauty consumption and counterfeit consumption to exemplify some of the harms generated from the conformity to the norms and values of late-capitalist consumer culture.

In Chapter 6, I turn my attention to the role of social media, focusing on how daily absorption in the virtual world impacts young people's sense of objective reality. Within this, I explore how social media provides young people with heightened exposure to unrealistic images and never-ending opportunities for hyper-comparison, alongside the real-life consequences this has on risky beauty consumption patterns. Chapter 7 turns to how hyper-comparison among female friends takes place in real-life settings. The first half of this section focuses on the Botox parties and how consuming beauty together was vital for the 'Clique', a female friendship group of beauty consumers. The second half turns to the Clique's intense fashion and beauty regimes, which took place before the 'big night out'. Chapter 8 concludes the book by drawing these issues together. This chapter summarizes the main findings and arguments to paint a picture of some of the harms associated with the market to work towards safeguarding the public against harm.

2

Contemporary Subjectivity and Hyper-Comparison

Introduction

In this chapter the ontological and epistemic underpinning of this book will be explored. Ultra-realist criminology and its transcendental materialist roots of subjectivity and zemiology will be introduced to provide a framework for understanding the multi-faceted cultural and corporeal motivations for buying, selling and using counterfeit illicit beauty products and services. Raymen and Smith's (2019) deviant leisure perspective that follows ultra-realism's ontological roots will also be outlined and its relevance to assess harms arising from the industry will be made clear. By drawing on these theoretical frameworks, the pernicious interconnection between the increasingly unstable and fluid job market, a culture of hyper-competitive consumer capitalism and hyper-comparison will be unpacked to better understand the research participants' involvement in illicit markets.

Ultra-realism, subjectivity and motivation

Liberal capitalism often leads us to believe that we are self-aware, logical and autonomous individuals who freely choose to act in our best self-interest without regard for others. Such a conceptualization of the individual as having pure agency and consciously entering the nexus of social, economic and political relationships comprising 'society' fails to engage with the complexity of human subjectivity and the unequal distribution of resource and opportunity. In failing to consider this complexity it is impossible to fully grasp how and why individuals continually and knowingly engage with a consumer culture that perpetuates harm for themselves, for others and for our shared environment.

There are enough media reports, celebrities, television documentaries and campaigns criticizing the beauty, fashion, diet and fitness industries to make us aware that such industries, albeit often marketed to increase happiness and wellbeing, are not geared towards empowering us. Rather, they thrive by making us continually compare ourselves, feel worse about ourselves and feel inadequate by creating a sense of lack about our appearances, our bodies and our self-worth. As the empirical data throughout this book will demonstrate, instead of rejecting these industries we are continuing to fuel their growth by constantly updating our beauty, fitness and diet regimes and consuming the latest products and services that 'promise' a new and improved self. In 2022, consumers spent $5.6 trillion on wellness products and services, up by 14 per cent from 2019, with the personal care and beauty, healthy eating, nutrition and weight loss markets estimated to account for 38.6 per cent of all wellness economy spending worldwide (Global Wellness Institute, 2023).

Ultra-realist criminology

Ultra-realist criminology emerged as a response to mainstream criminology's failure to explore causation and motivation and address the broader social, economic and political contexts in which crime occurs (Hall and Winlow, 2015). The perspective draws on various criminological traditions, including left realism, victimology, feminist criminology and critical realism (Kotzé and Lloyd, 2022) and it is particularly influenced by Roy Bhaskar's (1997) critical realist framework. It provides a new way of conceptualizing and explaining motivations for harmful behaviour.

The concept of 'harm' has been instrumental in criminal law, which typically has focused on 'identifying the causation of harm to others as a basis for restricting individual conduct, and for protecting individual rights vis-à-vis the state' (Copson, 2018: 48). Influenced by the broader zemiological shift within criminology (Pemberton, 2015; Kotzé, 2018), ultra-realism seeks to understand the reality of the harms inflicted upon victims from criminal and deviant practices. Therefore, going beyond the focus upon the individual culpability for harm, this perspective explores the social determinants of harm. This, of course, is not to dismiss individual responsibility for individual actions that lead to harm, but there needs to be an understanding of where the responsibility for those harms falls. This is an important issue to address when exploring counterfeiting, as many anti-counterfeiting arguments tend to place the onus on consumer responsibility. Therefore, the integration of a zemiological examination of the counterfeit and illicit beauty industry will ensure that when people are held responsible for their behaviours, they are only responsible for their behaviours and not the circumstances that underpin them (Copson, 2018).

Furthermore, a deviant leisure perspective, which seeks to investigate the harms linked to commodified forms of leisure, has been developed on the philosophical and theoretical foundations provided by ultra-realism. It is concerned more with the harms intrinsic to leisure activities and consumer industries, such as the lifestyle drug trade, the night-time economy (NTE), the growth of fitness and gym cultures and the everyday harms of social media within the context of consumer capitalism.[1] The deviant leisure perspective offers a highly pertinent theoretical framework for exploring beauty consumerism and how beauty use and supply is conformist and plays a vital role in surviving within the contemporary context of consumer capitalism.

Smith and Raymen (2018) suggest that it is essential to make distinctions between illegal leisure and leisure that is spatially contingent and legal but harmful, with the latter being categorized into four broad categories: subjective harms, environmental harms, socially corrosive harms and embedded harms. It would, however, be problematic to categorize the use and supply of counterfeit beauty as a form of illegal leisure. This is because the beauty market encompasses a range of legal, illegal, illicit and grey area products that are widely distributed online and offline. However, the harms associated with the beauty industry depend on a range of legal and regulatory frameworks that differ according to the type of product, country of origin and destination. Moreover, the illicit beauty market and its related harms have become normalized through its relationship and position alongside other leisure practices that contribute to contemporary circuits of capital accumulation. Smith and Raymen's (2018) categorization of harmful leisure can, therefore, be extended to include the diverse range of harms and risks associated with the industry across legal and illegal boundaries.

By recognizing subjective experiences of harm and exploring the underlying motivations driving harmful behaviour, ultra-realism aims to provide a more comprehensive understanding of harm. A central aspect of the ultra-realism perspective is, as Lloyd (2018: 247) notes, 'its capacity to interpret absences as well as presences'. It draws upon radical developments in philosophy and psychoanalysis to understand subjectivity and how it operates within its socio-economic context. In doing so, it employs an advanced conception of harm to examine the realities of our times and explain *why individuals self-harm and inflict harm on others and the environment in the pursuit of their own self-interest* (Hall and Winlow, 2015); this is where an ultra-realist perspective makes the most crucial contribution to this project.

An ultra-realist perspective offers a reconceptualized approach of subjectivity that seeks to facilitate a deeper understanding of the issues of transgression and conformity (Hall and Winlow, 2015). As opposed to Marx's claim that capitalist ideology is a false consciousness in which we act without awareness, ultra-realism utilizes Žižek's (2008) concept of the 'reversal of ideology' and his related process of *fetishistic disavowal,* where we collectively repress inconvenient or uncomfortable information, resulting in a form of ideological cynicism. Underlying this concept is the idea that we are aware of the harms of consumer culture but refuse to fully embrace this information, allowing us to continue as if we were unaware of the consequences and damage caused by our actions. This embodies what Pfaller (2017) termed as *interpassivity*, where individuals delegate their responsibilities and duty to make significant changes to their lives to external bodies and representative agents. This can be seen in action in numerous social situations where individuals might change the subject when political controversy arises or problems of our current climate are brought up (Hall and Winlow, 2015). As Raymen and Smith (2019: 29) point out:

> We watch the news and see that climate change is on the agenda. We are told to celebrate this and decry the pollution that consumerism is doing to our planet. In doing so, we are convinced that we are not the uninformed and duped masses. Our minds and beliefs have not been captured by consumer capitalism and we are glad that people are buying reusable coffee cups and that documentaries that speak 'truth to power' are being made about the realities of climate change. All of this critique and knowledge is not only tolerated but also actively encouraged.

The fact that we continue to engage in harmful patterns of consumption, such as buying 'fast fashion' and beauty products, goods with excess plastic packaging or booking annual holidays abroad, is an example of how we fetishistically disavow this uncomfortable information as if we are not cognizant of the harms generated by these industries. As we will come to see in Chapters 4 to 7, this idea of fetishistic disavowal was embodied by the research participants, who continued their harmful behaviour not because they were unaware of the harmful excesses that permeate the beauty industry, but because they were able to act as if they did not know about them. To therefore understand the reasons for engaging in this process, we need to acquire a more advanced understanding of subjectivity and the processes through which the subject comes into being.

Many of the key theoretical paradigms that inform much of social science tend to overlook and simplify the intricate nature of human subjectivity (Winlow, 2019). While only a few scholars have claimed that we do not possess an unconscious mind, sociological and criminological theories inexplicably continue to fail to include the unconscious in their conceptualizations of subjectivity, that is, to explore how drives and desires function within current socio-economic contexts to shape human actions. Transcendental materialism offers opportunities for social scientists to understand human actions and behaviour as it considers the formative emergence of the subject, focusing on the unconscious drives, desires and experiences.

Transcendental materialism

The foundation of transcendental materialism is based upon Žižek's incorporation of the Lacanian structure of the human psyche. Lacan's (1997) work builds upon and adapts Freud's concept of the id, ego and superego to create his own three interconnected structures of the psyche, which are regarded as orders or stages: the Real, the Imaginary and the Symbolic.

Contrary to other theoretical perspectives which situate the subject as either good but oppressed or innately dangerous and in need of control, within the heart of the Lacanian subject lies a void. The Lacanian perspective conceptualizes this as the Real, which plays a fundamental role in defining and shaping pre-symbolic subjective psychological experiences. Drawing on Fink's (1995: 24) example, the Real is an infant's body 'before' it is influenced by the Symbolic Order, 'before it is subjected to toilet training and instructed in the ways of the world'; it exists before the symbolism that permeates social and cultural life. For Lacan, this is where the subject is left in a state of confusion and desperately attempts to make sense of their current reality. The subject is imposed with terrifying feelings of conflict, terror, fear and is therefore desperate to break free from the constraints of the Real and enter into the Symbolic Order. All subjects are driven by a desire for completeness and coherence as they seek to pass through the Real and the Imaginary to reach the Symbolic Order and achieve socialization and a stable sense of the self (Lacan, 1997).

Nevertheless, before entering the Symbolic realm, the subject is required to go through the constant misidentifications inherent in the Imaginary. According to Lacan, the Imaginary Order is the mirror stage where the ego is formed by identifying with some spectral counterpart in the external world. It is a realm of susceptibility and self-deception, in which the subject constantly misrecognizes the self in the mirror image and their perception of reality does not reflect their lived reality, thereby making it impossible to attain (Raymen, 2018). The constant misidentifications result in the Imaginary Order being an intermittent source of dissatisfaction. In this sense, we can see how consumer capitalism prospers off the persistent misidentifications with the idealized lifestyle identities of consumer culture, whereby the insidious machination of marketing industries and the pressures to conform to ever-changing fashion trends intervene and continue to do so (Hall et al, 2008). Dissatisfaction is energized into desire by consumer capitalism's inescapable and suffocating marketing industries; objects become imbued with an almost mystical lifestyle symbolism, where the acquisition of these objects become essential for satisfaction and attaining the 'good' life. This is what McGowan (2016: 11) refers to as the 'promise' of capitalism. This concept is based on the idea that true satisfaction lies in the next purchase, trapping consumers in a cycle of desire and dissatisfaction.

Clear examples of this were found across the participants, with noticeable attempts to construct identities aligned to the fantasy images of ideal perfection (Chapter 6) and entrepreneurial success (Chapter 4) presented via social media, mass media and marketing tools in consumer culture. However, trapped within the Imaginary Order, their constant misidentification became a source of trauma and frustration that did not reflect their lived reality. Elle (23), for example, spoke candidly about her frustration:

> I try so hard to look like the glamorous people you see on *Love Island* and Instagram. You know, slim, tanned, white teeth. If I've had my hair done or Botox or something, I always try and take a nice photo. Because when you think you look good, you want to take selfies to upload [onto social media]. It's what people judge you on, isn't it? People see more of you on social media than in real life these days. But the photos never come out as good as I want them to. I'm just never happy with how I look in them. It's frustrating because it makes me get more work done and motivates me to keep improving myself until I'm happy with how I look.

Craig (24) reported a similar scenario as he attempted to shape his identity based on the fictitious image of 'the successful entrepreneur'. He discussed the frustration of not being able to materialize the same image:

> It's hard because I try and portray myself as an entrepreneur. But because I still work at the bar, it's like deep down I know I'm not one. It's all a bit fake really. An entrepreneur definitely doesn't work in a bar; they wear nice suits and drive fancy cars. It's frustrating because I'm trying hard to make something of myself. But I'm not giving up, it's just making me even more determined, so one day I can be.

The identity-orientated narcissism and individualism inherent in consumer capitalism steered the participants to seek out objects and signs of consumer culture in an attempt to construct their micro-identities and derive pleasure from these acquisitions. In striving to resemble the image of the 'successful entrepreneur' or of 'ideal perfection', both Elle and Craig gained a momentary sense of identity and coherence – but the full materialization of such identities is impossible as they are not emblematic of, and do not correspond with, their lived realities.

The failure to actualize their imagined identities prompted them to return to the pursuit of an unattainable image, thus keeping both Elle and Craig trapped within consumerism's Imaginary Order and unable to continue the journey of socialization from the Imaginary to the third of Lacan's orders, the Symbolic Order. Lacan maintains that the Symbolic Order defines and shapes our experience of everyday social life. It is not 'real' in any material sense, but it allows the subject to orient their life, shape a sense of self and understand the world around them. As Žižek (1997) observes, it merely exists because we behave as though it does; we are compelled by everyone else's subscription to its rules to act as if they believe in it. Postmodernism and the development of neoliberal capitalism have called into question the necessity of a coherent Symbolic Order which, as Raymen and Smith (2017: 388) contend, is 'hijacking the socialisation process and leaving individuals pursuing the unattainable specular images of aforementioned ego ideals presented in the external world'. Unable to escape the Imaginary realm, Lacan suggests that this entrapment results in narcissistic individualism – a characteristic that ultra-realists argue is indicative of late-capitalist subjectivity (Hall et al, 2008; Raymen, 2018).

Political economic restructure

But what relevance does this have with the consumption and supply of counterfeit and illicit beauty products? To bring this into contemporary context we can begin to see how discussions surrounding socio-economic and political change are reflected in the wider lived experiences of the working-class consumers and sellers in Beaufort. As Hall et al (2008) have argued, the emergence of the Thatcher government precipitated a fundamental shift in the construct of the social, where community bonds and ties have eroded. The traditional working-class communities and the collective identity and experiences grounded in locales were discarded to make way for post-industrial changes in favour of capital. The strategic intent to destroy valuable and important aspects of social life is encapsulated in Margret Thatcher's famous line that there was 'no such thing as a society, only individual men and women' (Harvey, 2007: 23). This was 'passed off by neoliberal ideologues as an act of "creative destruction" promising better things to come' (Hall et al, 2008: 4). Yet, this promise of 'better things' in a new era of freedom and prosperity was, for all but a limited number of elites, 'a sham' (Hall et al, 2008: 24). While the rich prospered, the working-class were atomized and left to live in uncertainty with increasingly unstable, part-time and precarious working and living conditions (Lloyd, 2013; Winlow and Hall, 2013; Winlow et al, 2017).

As we will come to see in Chapter 5, the flexibilization of labour under neoliberal capitalism has prompted a society of precariousness and uncertainty, and diminished the ability to make future plans. At the same time, it has destroyed any sense of collectivism and social solidarity, replacing it with a new culture of competitive individualism. Within this period, individuals were encouraged to view one another as a threat to job security and conspicuous consumption became a marker against which to assess their own value. While the autonomous self was allegedly liberated from the social bonds and structures of hierarchy that characterized industrial modernity, it heightened the need for a foundation upon which identity could be rooted. The 'world of consumer capitalism was happy to step into the void' (Raymen and Smith, 2019: 31) and provide socio-symbolic coherence as a means of escaping the terror of the Real. In a society of increased precariousness and individualism, we can begin to understand how we elicit an exaggerated adherence to the imaginary order of late capitalism. Therefore, the consumption and supply of illicit and counterfeit beauty products must be contextualized against the backdrop of economic austerity, the lack of legitimate labour opportunities available today, and in the context of the wider competitive and individualistic dynamics of consumer society.

Labour markets in late modernity

The legitimate employment opportunities available to the participants were limited, insecure and offered low wages. While it is needless to retell the story of the epochal shift from industrial capitalism to consumer capitalism, which is well-rehearsed elsewhere,[2] it is crucial to understand the connections between the rapid withdrawal of traditional forms of paid employment, and its major impact on young people's experience in the labour market across the UK, and the centrality of the leisure industry in shaping experiences of everyday life. As Winlow and Hall (2019: 24) stipulate, 'capitalism's ethos of aggressive competition has colonized almost every facet of life … everything that once seemed stable and reliable now seems to be on the verge of collapse as it is colonized by market logic'. This, of course, is not to suggest that the shift from industrial capitalism to consumer capitalism had the same impact on the southeast of England as it has on the northeast of England (Winlow and Hall, 2006; Lloyd, 2013; Raymen, 2018). However, the empirical data presented in this book confirms that the decline of legitimate forms of employment has had profound effects upon participants' first experience of paid labour at various levels.

Thorstein Veblen (2005: 7) suggests that 'the institution of leisure class is the outgrowth of an early discrimination between employments, according to which some employments are worthy and others unworthy'. However, this is perhaps more significant in the current context than ever before with the upsurge in zero-hour contracts and dead-end jobs (Standing, 2011; Friedman, 2014). The change and reconstitution of society have resulted in a sense of uncertainty and risk in an unstable and changing world. The previous norm of spending an entire working life in the same job is unlikely as the job market has become increasingly more unstable and fluid (Southwood, 2011). Individuals are living in a state of normalized precarity where work has become devoid of positive symbolism (see Lloyd, 2013). In particular, young people are increasingly experiencing excess pressures and anxieties, with the increase in university fees, decrease in employment stability and the precarity of Brexit (Hope, 2024). Before the economic collapse of 2008, individuals found themselves with more disposable income, easier access to credit and fundamentally less debt. However, since the financial crisis the UK has faced several economic challenges, leading to uncertain future prospects and a rise in unemployment and temporary employment, pushing many closer to a life riddled with debt (Davis and Cartwright, 2019).

Most of the participants in the study stepped into the early stages of adulthood during an era of post-crash capitalism, gaining first-hand experience of the effects of the decline in legitimate employment opportunities. The economic prospects of young people who have just left school or university and have entered the labour market full-time are poor. Across the participants, only one person was in a full-time, 9 to 5 job. Although most participants (aside from one) were in a form of employment throughout this study, such rates are by no means representative of the whole country; the unemployment rate for young people in the UK remains high, with 12 per cent of all people aged 16 to 24 not in education, employment or training (ONS, 2024). Of the participants that managed to secure work, many were forced to accept insecure, zero-hour, short-term contracts, without security of employment, leaving them with irregular hours and wages that fell below the National Living Wage (Hardgrove et al, 2015).[3] As a result, some were forced to work multiple jobs to overcome the limited employment opportunities that were incapable of providing them with a decent income.

In Dick Hobbs's (1988) historical research of entrepreneurship in the East End of London, *Doing the Business*, the pursuit of profit relied on 'keenness and vivacity' (Bermant, 1975: 23) to find a new form of employment and survive. Individuals were reliant on street vending and 'everyone was on the look-out for something to vend' (Bermant, 1975: 23) to 'chisel a niche for oneself' (Hobbs, 1998: 123). This form of entrepreneurialism can still be seen in contemporary society, with a rise in individuals actively seeking independent, self-employed and informal opportunities to generate more income that would be difficult to produce in the traditional labour market (Thieme, 2021). From social media influencing and beauty blogging to selling licit and illicit beauty products and services, the point surrounding survival remains the same three decades later. The young people in this study framed both their licit and illicit actions as necessary for economic and symbolic survival under neoliberalism. They understood the stark and brutal realities of social exclusion and social insignificance and attempted to put themselves in a better position by exploiting the limited opportunities around them. For some participants, this involved working in one of Britain's most low-sanctioned yet profitable industries (Antonopoulos et al, 2018). Selling counterfeit beauty was perceived as the only feasible option to earn a decent income and survive in increasingly insecure economic conditions. As was laid out in Chapter 1, the most common claim surrounding counterfeiting is that it is associated with 'wider criminality' and the profits from counterfeiting are used to fund other forms of crime. However, the total irrelevance between legitimate and illegitimate money was a recurring theme throughout this research project.[4] As such, selling counterfeits was a way to supplement legitimate work in response to the inadequacies (what Fagan and Freeman, 1999, termed 'doubling up on their income') and perceived financial shortcomings in the legitimate economy.

Participants all remained committed to selling counterfeits throughout the entire duration of the fieldwork and viewed their actions as a means to survive in a culture where employment opportunities were few, insecure and poorly paid. David (28), for example, sold counterfeits as a means to deal with the 'ferocious financial world', a world that is 'dominated by hypocrisy and throat-cutting competition' (Ruggiero and South, 1995: 179). He sold counterfeit perfumes to provide for his child and move away from drug dealing. Life events such as having a child can put significant pressure on drug dealers like David to switch to less risky markets, even if the financial gains are lower in the short term. In this respect, there is evidence of a transition from drug dealing to counterfeit selling (McCartney, 2005), although by no means do those involved in drug markets all become counterfeit sellers. Selling counterfeit perfumes appeared to be the only feasible option to supplement his part-time wage in the hospitability industry. It was considered to be more culturally accepted as it received few, if not zero, penalties, making opportunities for counterfeit selling easier and more appealing. Personal circumstances, life experiences, the extent of policing, the social acceptability of the illicit product, and attitudes towards harm and crime were all found to influence decisions to sell illicit goods (Antonopoulos, 2007; Hall et al, 2008; Antonopoulos et al, 2011).

Participant accounts were, thus, symptomatic of the way in which capitalism cultivates conditions in which individuals willingly 'risk harm to others as they pursue their instrumental and expressive interests' (Hall and Winlow, 2018: 43). At a proximate level of explanation, the primary driver of counterfeit selling was the potential to make money in low-risk markets. Income derived was seen to fulfil a number of functions in young people's lives: it aided David to remain sheltered and support his family; it provided some with a way of financing luxury bars and clubs within the 'alluring'; it supplemented legitimate incomes to generate the surplus income required to indulge in their penchant for designer items and the latest consumer goods without putting themselves in excessive debt; and it enabled some to strengthen social bonds among friends and peers. Therefore, rather than an alternative to legitimate employment, illicit markets were used as a financial safety net to stabilize income during times of economic instability or hardship.

While existing literature has focused on counterfeiting in relation to harm and frames it as a crime, most of the sellers, albeit to different extents, sold counterfeits to buy consumer items and construct themselves as a successful consumer, increase their popularity as a seller to secure more work, increase their popularity as a consumer, and, ultimately, to fund and expand their consumer lifestyles. David, however, was diametrically different from the other sellers as he had an obligation to support his family financially. The other sellers sold counterfeits to fund a lifestyle that is primarily marked by excessive and wasteful luxury consumption, as they appeared to 'buy (the time of) their lives' (Žižek, 2014: 5). They understood there was a 'game of getting rich by entrepreneurial means' (Hall et al, 2008: 54). This absence of stability and security thus reflected individual motivations to harm, and embodied the contemporary entrepreneurial spirit to commit both legal and illegal acts with the potential for personal gain at the expense of the wellbeing of others. Involvement in illicit selling, therefore, reflected a commitment to what Hall (2012b) identifies as the realm of 'special liberty', where sellers pursued their individualistic desires, however harmful to others, without regard for the wellbeing of others and with minimal opposition or restraint.

The centrality of leisure and consumption

Following significant changes across economic, social, political and technological dimensions over the last few decades, consumerism and leisure have become dominant forces shaping everyday life (Bauman, 2007). The shift from industrialism to consumerism resulted in large consequences for both labour markets and work cultures in Britain, altering the balance between labour and social life in Britain (Rojek, 2010; Cederström and Fleming, 2012). As a result, cities and towns have undergone significant change, transitioning from being centred around production to now revolving around leisure and consumption. This cultural transformation has contributed to the creation of a generation that identifies with the pursuit of hedonistic pleasures like never before (see Smith, 2014). Both consumerism and leisure have become an integral part of contemporary culture and play a dominant role in shaping the desires, fantasies and aspirations of consumers. Thus, not only has this societal shift caused dire consequences of precarious employment and a breakdown in social relations, but it has also played a large role in increasing pressures and anxieties intrinsically linked to consumption practices and participation in leisure activities to gain a clear social standing and identity.

Both consumption and leisure have become a form of labour (Rojek, 2010) and the freedom and vitality that was once a feature of society has now developed into increased pressures, anxieties and challenges. Fisher (2009), for example, advocates that the lack of a sense of financial and employment security, and the pressure to adopt a particular lifestyle, contributes towards the vast amount of mental health disorders such as anxiety and depression. Further, as Hayward (2004: 152) remarks: 'late modern society is often characterised in terms of a pervasive sense of insecurity and disembeddedness: not just in the well-documented areas of cultural production and declining industrial capitalism, but also, importantly, in the realms of everyday life and at the level of individual consciousness and awareness.' As such, the consumption of appearance and the intense pressure to consume operates against a social and economic backdrop characterized by competitive individualism, hyper-comparison, precarity and objectless anxiety that embodies neoliberal capitalism.

One of the most compelling explanations of the role and function of consumption and leisure is seen in Thorstein Veblen's (2005) work in *The Theory of the Leisure Class.* Veblen (2005) theorized and analysed the social functions and characteristics of individuals and their relationship to leisure and aimed to understand their underlying drives and motivations. His theory centres on the notion that motivations of leisure were a symbolic display of 'conspicuous consumption'. Veblen (2005) infers that 'conspicuous consumption' permeated society through what he terms 'pecuniary emulation'. He categorizes the upper classes as the 'leisure class' and suggests that an individual's status within society depends on 'pecuniary strength', which is reflected when one lives a life of leisure through 'conspicuous consumption' (Veblen, 2005: 47). As a result, the 'leisure class' were deemed as those with a high status; they were a privileged class within society that had economic power and freedom. Hall et al (2008: 90) note:

> For Veblen, the purpose of conspicuous displays of consumption was to indicate a high status that separates the individual from the practical dimension of social necessity; but it's not the ownership of the goods that counts, or indeed the benefits they might provide, it's the knowledge that they have been obtained by means other than manual work, which of course, implies that at some point in the process of acquisition everyday moral boundaries might well have been transgressed.

Veblen suggests that the leisure class engaged in conspicuous hedonistic leisure pursuits, which he argued as being fundamentally wasteful and indulgent. In contemporary society, luxury beauty and fashion brands have shifted from being the domain of the upper classes and have become increasingly available to the emerging middle classes as potential consumers of luxury items through their increased income and subsequent demands for such luxury brands (Bauman, 2011). For example, Botulinum toxin (Botox) – 'once a luxury item only available to elites' (Hall, 2019: 175) – is now 'run-of-the-mill' as it is relatively affordable, easily accessible in familiar environments, and as important as other regular body upkeep practices such as teeth cleaning, haircuts and having a manicure (Berkowitz, 2017; Cook and Dwyer, 2017; Hall, 2019). This indicates that class matters less today. Rather, individual differentiation and the ability to display status through consumption and leisure has become a signifier and plays a fundamental role in the hierarchy of admiration and identity creation. As we will see in Chapter 7, individuals compared their affluence and position in society in relation to others, with leisure serving as an important space for validating and denoting this differentiation. Therefore, the continuous pursuit of goods is the standard of social differentiation and is what Veblen argues as evidence of pecuniary strength.

Such changes in the global economic landscape have aided the democratization of leisure that goes beyond what Veblen (2005) terms as the 'leisure class'. The consumption of fashion and beauty in contemporary society has become a fundamental component of commodified leisure pursuits that occur in both physical and virtual spaces. Leisure spaces such as social media platforms, fitness spaces and the NTE are clearly geared around the promotion and construction of the self and offer a space for self-presentation as individuals compete for attention. As such, it is important to examine the deeply embedded conformity of beauty within other forms of leisure, to analyse the drives and motivations, and consider how it emerges from broader cultural and economic structures.

Existing literature on late modernity has recognized how beauty and fashion are intrinsically linked to other forms of leisure, which is encapsulated quite succinctly by what Jason Kelly (2016) refers to as 'the new economy of mind and body'. Kelly (2016) delves into the subcultures that drive the elusive world of exercise and its relationship with the 'quantified self'. Kelly (2016) illustrates the extent to which individuals are willing to pay to keep up with the fitness industry, which has become an increasingly large part of people's social identity. Although fitness pursuits are not unique to late capitalism, they have been further capitalized through the emergence of 'fitness fashion', fashionable fitness wear, sweat-proof beauty products, and fitness restaurants and cafes such as The Skinny Kitchen, which not only offer the latest 'clean eating trends' but also an arena to display 'athleisure' wear. Gyms and fitness studios have transformed from being a place to just work out to places that have cult followings – one such example being the Skinny Bitch Collective, an exclusive invitation-only cult training practice which garnered a cult-like following in the mid 2010s. Additionally, there has also been an emergence of facial workout training, with FaceGym offering workouts and toning exercises specifically for the face. Accordingly, beauty consumption and its attachment of social significance to leisure has the capacity to hold illustrious meanings and values (Large, 2019). The conspicuous consumption of beauty brands provides consumers with status symbols that can communicate their wealth, social status and identity. Thus, leisure and consumption have become a fundamental component of contemporary culture, intrinsically connected to aspects of identity and lifestyle, creating cynicism and narcissistic competition through hyper-comparison.

Moreover, for Bauman (2007), the idea of the consumer society relies on the notion that 'social identity' is acquired through the display of consumer items and commodified experiences. Drawing on Bauman's (2007) work, Raymen and Smith (2016: 397) note that 'consumer society demands that "social identity" is attainable only through accepting the market as a source of self-determination which insists that those at the bottom of the pile should be vilified'. Consumers are now caught up in the increasing pressure to flaunt iconic and recognizable brand logos to compete and keep up with new trends as they appear. Therefore, in the words of Presdee (2001: 60), society is based on the notion that 'without consumption there can be no social life and no social identity'.

Such commitment to consumerism, underpinned by what Žižek (2002) describes as the 'cultural injunction to enjoy', undermines concerns regarding the potential harms inflicted on others. Žižek (2002) advocates that the 'injunction to enjoy' compels individuals to seek out enjoyment. He claims that if the individual fails to actively enjoy these opportunities of indulgence and hedonistic excess, guilt will reside within the individual. As we will come to see in Chapter 6, such pressure is amplified by the threat of cultural obsolescence and the fear of missing out (FOMO) that individuals experience when they are unable to keep up with the latest trends and experiences (Raymen and Smith, 2019), creating an 'objectless anxiety' (Hall, 2012a). Winlow and Hall (2009: 94) encapsulate the interaction between consumerism, leisure cultures and identity as being 'obligatory and laden with risk, anxiety and chronic dissatisfaction at the deepest psychological level'. As such, we can see how the consumption of beauty and appearance is 'fundamentally expected' of an individual (Hayward, 2004: 161). While consumers are sold ideals of identity and freedom through beauty, cosmetics and grooming products, the reality is that the nature of beauty is structurally and systemically harmful.

Such harms are seen within consumer capitalism's simultaneous cultivation of feelings of absence, desire and dissatisfaction (Lacan, 2007). As Bauman (1992: 225) points out, consumerism fails to deliver on its promise:

> It actually promises universality of happiness. Everybody is free to choose, and, if everybody is let into the shop, then everybody is equally happy. That is one duplicity. Another duplicity is the limitation of its pretence that you resolve the issue of freedom completely once you offer a consumer freedom. So it is a reduction of freedom to

> consumerism. That is the other duplicity. People are led into forgetting that there could also be other ways of self-assertion than simply buying a better outfit.

Consumers are continuously urged to purchase the 'new', which creates a perpetual feeling of dissatisfaction with the 'old'. However, the 'new' is changing so rapidly that the new is already old, which arguably leads to a 'culture of eternal dissatisfaction' (Passini, 2013: 370): an endless pursuit of want in which fulfilment is replaced by the endless search for it (Campbell, 1989; Passini, 2013). Rosenthal (2005: 43) suggests that the 'ever-increasing consumption is counteracted by "hedonic adaption", in which we need ever-higher quantities to obtain the same boost in satisfaction' and describes this as being like an addiction for many. Therefore, the pressure to conform to consuming in society indicates how individuals are at a certain risk of binge-consuming behaviours (Passini, 2013). As Hayward and Hobbs (2007: 444) note, 'the insatiability of desire has been regarded as a symptom of a certain moral pathology (be it sin or decadence) or as a sign of status among social elites'. However, a distinctive feature of the late-modern consumer culture is that this insatiable desire is not only normalized, but it is vital for the continuance of the socio-economic order (Baudrillard, 1996; Bauman, 1998; Hayward and Hobbs, 2007).

Hyper-comparison as a driving force

This social and economic backdrop of neoliberalism is also accompanied by scarce and precarious employment opportunities that drive aggressive competition and symbolic violence into the social body (Taylor, 2013). The hyper-connectedness between work and leisure, online and offline spheres, and consumers and sellers are central to understanding contemporary forms of harm. Such hyper-connectedness affords new material opportunities and shapes the contemporary beauty industry, driving demand and profoundly altering subjective experiences. Except for David, all the sellers in this study were driven by an unwavering commitment to the ethos of hyper-consumption. Their motivations for selling illicit goods were no different to those who worked in legitimate jobs, and they described their income through selling illicit goods as a means to consume their desired body and lifestyle. This in turn meant they could gain more work (in both legal and illegal markets) as well as increase their popularity among peers and friends (both online and in real life). Ryan (26), for example, saw his appearance as vital for selling cars and both Sophie (25) and Olivia (25) used their appearances to help sell and promote products through social media, and ultimately, increase their social media following. This dual approach of selling counterfeits while working legitimate jobs ensured the continuation of 'symbolic security' (Tudor, 2019) for the research participants, enabling them to compete within the hyper-comparative and competitive individualistic environment.

The development of this form of hyper-comparison is inextricably connected with the cultural changes and technological advances occurring within the landscape of late capitalism. As noted in this chapter, narcissism, competitive individualism and profound insecurity lay at the heart of existence in contemporary Western neoliberal society. The engagement in harmful consumption practices was a means for the participants to avoid their own cultural obsolescence (discussed in Chapter 5). Such an avoidance was seen as a fundamental part of their success in contemporary society. As Treadwell et al (2013: 8) remark:

> Consumerism, indulgence and excess are the markers of a good and successful life, and failure to be actively and continually involved in this symbolic realm reflects cultural irrelevance and an absence of life. This means of achieving an identity is so precious yet so precarious that the subjects themselves have decided that failure cannot be tolerated.

This fear of failure and its surrounding anxieties drove the participants towards potentially harmful acts so as to avoid the unimaginable: an inability to consume goods and experiences, to display their superfluities, and to become culturally irrelevant. Building on consumer capitalism's 'promise', I argue here that hyper-comparison is at the heart of contemporary society and acts as a catalyst behind young people's willingness to inflict harm on the self, on others and on their environments. As discussed earlier in this chapter, the psychoanalytical roots of consumerism suggest that human desire is not solely about the enjoyment that is derived from the acquisition of commodities. Instead, consumer capitalism is predicated upon the failure to find satisfaction. The system perpetually instils dissatisfaction in consumers who demand new, better, faster experiences and commodities, and who become trapped in an eternal cycle of searching for the 'new' (Bauman, 2007). As such, the promises of consumer capitalism to meet the demands of its subjects are never met and remain perpetually unfulfilled. This results in the subject not deriving satisfaction from what they believe they desire, but perversely finding 'satisfaction in repeating loss' (McGowan, 2016: 28). Crucially, the constant hyper-comparison between consumer subjects further drives feelings of inadequacy, dissatisfaction and absence (Lacan, 2007), and as subjects find themselves repeatedly cheated of the 'promises' of consumption they turn to potentially more harmful products and experiences to avoid their cultural obsolescence and social oblivion.

As contemporary life is now entirely organized around consumption (Bauman, 2007), young people are constantly flooded with material possessions. Such audiences are bombarded with advertisements and media that celebrate the consumer capitalist ideals of competition and individualism (Irwin-Rogers, 2019), perpetuating the experiences of hyper-comparison. Many brands frame themselves in terms of a successful lifestyle and material wealth. For instance, Rolex attempts to encourage potential consumers to celebrate their successes with the purchase of 'a crown for every achievement' and brands such as L'Oréal and Nike have embedded their well-known slogans, 'Because you're worth it' and 'Just do it', into the minds of consumers. With global campaigns promoting the idea that achievements should be celebrated with an expensive purchase, it was no surprise that participants equated their self-worth and value with the products and brands they could acquire and display to others. Clearly then, the relationship between hyper-comparison and desire plays a significant role in both perpetuating consumption and exacerbating the absence of satisfaction within an individual.

As the empirical data from this book uncovers, the issue of hyper-comparison and competition was central to understanding the way in which the participants explained their readiness to self-harm and harm others. Although the sellers in this study highlighted the centrality of money for their actions, they were keen to stress that if they could not earn money within illicit markets, they would have taken on additional debt rather than fall down the economic and social ladder. This willingness to take on further debt was evident in the accounts of all participants who suggested that their incomes from the legitimate labour markets prevented them from achieving the success that others around them were experiencing. The seductive symbolism of the latest designer products is partially responsible for this as consumers are lured with promises that consuming such material goods will address their physical and social inadequacies and insecurities. For many young people, if they cannot acquire a Rolex or accumulate enough money to buy a product with symbolic value, it is taken as a direct sign of failure. Although this is far from new, and capitalist consumerism has long encouraged people to prioritize relationships with objects over subjects (Žižek, 2006), it has been heightened by the way in which social media mediates FOMO and hyper-comparison.

Chapter summary

This chapter has presented the ontological and epistemic frameworks of this monograph. After highlighting some of the critiques with the current landscape of criminological theory, ultra-realist criminology was introduced as a means of overcoming current issues with existing criminological theory. Through an account of Lacanian psychoanalysis and a conceptualization of contemporary subjectivity, the chapter has provided an understanding of how the conditions of contemporary neoliberal capitalism and consumer culture cultivate harmful and competitive individualistic subjectivities. It follows ultra-realism's call to 'return to motivation' to understand why individuals are willing to harm themselves, others and their environments in their pursuit of ideological image and body perfection.

The second part of this chapter introduced the wider environment in which the subject comes into being. It examined the shifts in the socio-economic landscape that have led to the ascendancy of neoliberal capitalism as a way of organizing the economy. This economic and political restructuring has had dire consequences for employment, social relations and identity. The hyper-connectedness of consumers and sellers, work and leisure and online and offline spheres are all central to understanding contemporary forms of harm. This is not only due to the material opportunities they provide but also because of the way they profoundly reshape human experience and subjectivity. Finally, the concept of hyper-comparison was introduced.

Overall, this chapter has illustrated the significance of the socio-economic landscape shaping the economic behaviour and subjective experiences of participants. It underscores how harm is entwined with broader processes of consumerism, highlighting the importance of critically examining global consumer culture and political change. In forging strong theoretical connections between harmful actions and wider economic, social and cultural forces, structures and processes, we can begin to understand young people's willingness to sell and buy beauty counterfeits, and to inflict harm on themselves and others.

3

The Changing Nature of Beauty, Enhancement and Harm

Introduction

Having introduced the theoretical frameworks of this book, the following chapter provides a theorization of the changing nature of beauty, style and fashion. Various historical and contemporary normalized, accepted and culturally celebrated harmful and harming practices will be explored, emphasizing how fashion and style have long shown a connection with harmful and harming practices. Following this, an examination of how late modernity has accelerated and amplified the harmful and harming practices and processes related to the use and supply of beauty and fashion will be unpacked, highlighting the extent to which potential harms exist on a larger scale than previously recognized. As such, this chapter continues to explore the hyper-connectedness of consumers and sellers and the online and offline.

A history of fashion trends and harmful practices

Fashion before neoliberalism

Fashion and style have been an integral part of human culture for centuries. While trends are constantly changing and vary across cultures, the extent to which individuals will go to stay abreast with new styles has been consistent throughout history and dates back to periods preceding the dominance of neoliberal ideology (David, 2015). From fashionable clothing that has led to mechanical alterations and modifications of the natural body, to extreme dieting to achieve a certain body shape, individuals have long engaged in practices that can cause significant harm to the self and the broader societal and environmental landscapes.

Fashion trends have traditionally been heavily gendered, with certain styles and body shapes associated with masculinity and femininity (Grogan, 2022). This has led individuals to mechanically alter their natural body within and across historical periods and cultural contexts. For example, significant fashion-related health risks for women can be dated back to the thirteenth century, when foot-binding to restrict normal growth was a cultural phenomenon among young girls in China (Cummings et al, 1997). While women with bound feet were a symbol of beauty, femininity and social status that allowed them to be married into money, this cultural practice had harmful consequences for individuals, impacting balance, the ability to walk and causing severe pain and deformity (Levy, 1966). Additionally, from the sixteenth century to the early twentieth century, corsets began to gain popularity among the affluent social class in the Western world. These were fashionable garments worn by individuals to shape the body into a desired silhouette. From the nineteenth century to the early twentieth century, corset wearing was at its highest, and discussions surrounding the health risks began to gain attention. Corsets of this time were made using either bone or metal inserts which allowed the waist to be tightly constricted to create the hourglass figure in the 1800s and the 'S' figure in the 1900s (Steele, 2001). However, sustained pressure on the ribs, waists and lungs were inherently dangerous and caused significant health issues such as difficulties breathing, indigestion and internal bleeding. In some cases, this also caused the movement of other internal organs and death, with reports suggesting that pieces of steel from corsets were found in the heart (*New York Times*, 1903).

While women have faced significant risks and discomfort through beauty practices to conform to certain trends, men have also risked their lives for the sake of fashion. An example of this can be seen during the nineteenth and the early twentieth century, when Edwardian men would wear 'stiff collars' as a fashion accessory to add a touch of formality to their attire. While they were designed to add structure and support, prolonged wearing of stiff collars could cause some men to experience discomfort and irritation around the neck. They were known as 'father killers', with some men suffocating from the high and stiff nature of the collars (*New York Times*, 1888). Therefore, although there were distinct standards and expectations for men and women, both men and women have willingly engaged with harmful practices over the centuries for the sake of fashion and beauty, prioritizing short-term aesthetic gain over long-term health. Such expectations to meet standards have led women to continuously attempt to look like what they thought women should look like, and men to continuously attempt to look like what they thought men should look like, despite the potential harms involved in the practices associated with their pursuit of gendered ideals (Grogan, 2022).

Exploitation in the fashion industry

Alongside the physical alteration of the body driven by harmful clothing, there have also been various harms to the makers of fashion items (David,

2015). Fashion has long been intertwined with the exploitation of other human beings, including dangerous conditions endured by workers, the use of child labour and wage exploitation. Before the mass production of fashion and beauty products and services, wealthy individuals would wear handmade, bespoke garments and cosmetics, while the middle and lower classes often relied on ready-to-wear garments and homemade remedies using resources found in their immediate environment. These items, whether for the wealthy or middle to lower classes, were often made by skilled workers that worked long hours in poor conditions (David, 2015). While such occupational hazards before the industrial revolution may not have been as well-documented as those today, there were still many risks involved in producing fashion, including factors such as workplace conditions, chemical exposure and occupational diseases. One clear example of an occupational hazard in the eighteenth and nineteenth centuries can be seen in men's fashion, with the use of toxic substances such as mercury in the production of felt hats. This was termed the 'mad hatter disease', where mercury poisoning caused hat makers to experience tremors, pathological shyness and irritability (Waldron, 1983). Furthermore, in the Victorian era, seamstresses were required to sew for an excessive amount of time to meet tight deadlines, with little rest and no safety regulations in place. An example of the consequences of the harsh working conditions can be seen in the case of Mary Walkley, a seamstress who died after working for twenty-six and a half hours straight to complete an order (David, 2015). Although significant changes and advancements in workplace safety regulations have reduced the amount of harm experienced by workers, occupational hazards in the fashion and beauty industry can still be seen today (see Edwards, 2024).

Such harms were not just experienced by those making and consuming fashion; wider beauty practices also posed significant health risks to individuals. The willingness to conform to beauty standards and engage in harmful practices that prioritized aesthetics over health and wellbeing can be found throughout history and across cultures (Jeffreys, 2014; David, 2015). Socialites in the eighteenth century exemplified this through their use of cosmetics with risky ingredients, such as lead to achieve a pale complexion by making the skin appear lighter. While the presence of lead and other heavy metal impurities in cosmetic products is now heavily regulated and monitored (Axford et al, 2023), the contemporary beauty industry continues to rely on a range of chemicals and potentially harmful substances in the production of cosmetics and other personal care products (see British Skin Foundation, 2023). Therefore, risk and harm have always been inherent in the pursuit and consumption of beauty and have been normalized in a variety of ways throughout history. Yet these harms take on a markedly different scale within contemporary society as a result of technological advancement and acceleration.

Technology and changes in fashion, beauty and harm

The processes of globalization and technological advancements have fundamentally changed the way fashion and beauty products and services are produced, distributed and sold. Large factories rapidly producing items to maximize profits, the development of global supply chains, outsourcing and access to ever cheaper labour and materials have all contributed to massive scales of production delivered on a just-in-time basis. This manufacturing philosophy of 'Global Quick Response' methods (MacCarthy and Jayarathne, 2010) has become increasingly popular among retailers, as companies try to keep up with new trends. Furthermore, advances in information communication technologies have significantly transformed the way we shop, communicate and consume.

The rise of the platform economy and the increasing accessibility and convenience of digital technologies and online financial activities has driven increased opportunities for 'business-to-business (B2B), business-to-consumer (B2C), and consumer-to-consumer (C2C) marketplaces with huge market reach' (Hall and Antonopoulos, 2016: 23). The upsurge in online marketplaces, social media platforms and dedicated blogs and forums have all expanded the opportunities for the discovery, sale and consumption of fashion and beauty. Consumers can share opinions, leave recommendations, and browse reviews about prospective brands, products and services before making their purchasing decisions. Developments and integrations between social media and shopping platforms (for example, 'Instagram Shopping' and 'TikTok Shop') further increase the convenience and accessibility for consumption, demonstrating the intimate link between technological developments and the shaping of the fashion and beauty industry.

The very nature of fashion and the body is inescapably connected with consumerism. With the emergence of mass production and dissemination of fashion items, notions of style and beauty have significantly transformed. According to cultural criminologists, style is deeply connected to individual and group identities, and it is rooted in the daily practices of social life:

> [It is] embedded in haircuts, posture, clothing, automobiles, music, and the many other avenues through which people present themselves publicly. But it is also located between people, and among groups; it constitutes an essential element in collective behaviour, an element whose meaning is constructed through the nuances of social interaction. (Ferrell, 1995: 170)

The hegemony of consumer culture is underpinned by the logics of 'self-improvement and self-expression', which influence all social groups

(Featherstone, 2007: 84), who are now faced with new pressures to conform to ever-changing fashion trends (Widdows, 2021). It has traditionally been suggested by cultural scholars that fashion styles could be understood as a means of 'resistance' (see Hall and Jefferson, 2006). Emblematic of such resistance is the skinhead movement of the 1960s and the punk fashion of the 1970s (Hebdige, 1979), both of which emerged from the marginalized experiences of working-class communities. Such trends and styles are accompanied with identities, tropes and perceptions that, in part, have historically been stigmatized in the media, where they are constructed as 'risky' or 'undesirable'. This can be seen in recent history through the preoccupation in certain media outlets that ascribe the wearing of the 'hoodie' as dangerous, threatening and a sign of criminality (see Treadwell, 2008). While the wearing of clothing and certain items of fashion can still be seen as counter-cultural, it is also a core part of everyday consumption, enabling individuals to express themselves, conform to cultural ideals and display their identity while simultaneously engaging in the pleasures of consumption (Hayward, 2004).

Harms in the twentieth and twenty-first centuries

In the post-war period, the profound transformations and rapid growth of the fashion and beauty industry prompted an increased focus on body image. As technological advancements and mass production made fashion and beauty more accessible, media outlets such as magazines, television and cinema played a key role in disseminating trends and creating more societal pressures to conform to an ideal body image. One example of this is when Christian Dior's 'New Look' emerged in the late 1940s, promoting a slim hourglass figure for women. The promotion of idealized body types such as these led to widespread body dissatisfaction and contributed to a rise in eating disorders and mental health issues (Offer, 2021) that, as we will come to see in Chapter 5, have persisted into the twenty-first century.

The relationship between fashion, beauty trends and harmful practices has continued and intensified further in the twenty-first century, particularly as social media platforms have amplified these unrealistic standards. Contemporary society's focus on the body has facilitated an even larger market in beauty and cosmetics, enabling consumers to manipulate their body in line with the latest trends, which are deeply rooted in the everyday practices of social life, with fad diets, cosmetic procedures, pharmaceuticals and grooming products. In particular, Botox, dermal fillers, teeth whitening kits, slimming products, skin tanning and lightening products, contact lenses and grooming products more generally have all seen substantial rises in popularity. However, this increased usage is accompanied by the emergence of additional anxieties, insecurities and further harm, as individuals continually engage in the consumption of such products in an attempt to keep pace with changing trends. Therefore, while the specific harms and dangers may have changed over the years, one thing remains the same: an obsession with how the body appears and performs.

A clear example of this is found within the popularization and increased use of lifestyle drugs and cosmetics for aesthetic enhancements. Lifestyle drugs encompass a wide range of medications consumed through personal choice to treat conditions or perceived deficiencies that are deemed as non-life threatening and not medically necessary, and these are often consumed in the pursuit of non-health-related goals rather than due to illness (Hall, 2019). As a sub-category of lifestyle drugs, image-enhancing drugs come in a variety of forms 'from drugs to tan or lighten the skin, products to stimulate hair growth or prevent hair loss and drugs to prevent wrinkles or smoothen skin' (Human Enhancement Drugs, 2017a). Alongside the growing popularity of legal beauty products and services, there has been an increase in individuals undergoing cosmetic surgery in the UK and of cosmetic surgery tourism. The British Association of Aesthetic Plastic Surgeons (BAAPS, 2023) reported that 31,057 cosmetic procedures took place in Britain in 2022, representing a 102 per cent rise compared to the previous year. Additionally, the politicization of Botox influences its accessibility and the locations where it can be administered, enabling it to emerge in new fields and places whereby it transcends medical control (Cook and Dwyer, 2017). Consequently, the consumption and supply of Botox is moving from traditional medical environments and practices into beauty salons, dentists, hairdressers and, as we will come to see in Chapter 4, to the comfort of the home through events such as Botox parties (Berkowitz, 2017; Cook and Dwyer, 2017). In this chapter we will meet Carys (28), one of the study participants, who offered Botox alongside her legitimate mobile hairdressing business and held Botox parties in the privacy of the home.

Self-governed, privatized healthcare and beauty regimes

This expansion in the consumption of illicit pharmaceuticals and cosmetic treatments outside of clinical settings by individuals without medical knowledge or experience is accompanied by a range of direct and indirect harms (Hall and Antonopoulos, 2016; Cook and Dwyer, 2017). Following the Western trends of desired body types through 'thinspiration' and 'fitspiration' (see Grogan, 2022), weight-loss drugs, diet pills and nutritional supplements are widespread across health and beauty markets in the UK. The purpose of weight-loss drugs and diet pills is to enhance weight loss by reducing the appetite and stimulating fat metabolism, leading to an overall reduction in body weight and body fat (Human Enhancement Drugs, 2017b).

Rises in individuals self-diagnosing and self-prescribing medications online have accompanied declining levels of trust in the National Health

Service (NHS) (Hall and Antonopoulos, 2016). While this presents new opportunities for individuals to supply, and consumers to purchase, illicit medicines online, Underhill (2008: 177) argues that people 'need to feel a certain level of confidence in a product and its value, which comes only from hard evidence, not from TV commercials or word of mouth'. However, 'slimming drugs' are widely available to consumers and there is clear evidence of their use and promotion through word of mouth among users of anorexia forums (see Sugiura et al, 2012). Acting upon such information, however, is fraught with danger, as can be seen with the rise of people using potentially falsified Saxenda and Ozempic injection pens for weight loss in the UK (MHRA, 2023). Such use of unregulated products can lead to adverse health conditions, hospitalization and deaths (see Walsh and Rai, 2023). Although some may argue that these products are not 'beauty' products per se, their capacity to alter an individual's appearance in hopes of achieving a specific aesthetic contributes to their relationship with beauty for consumers. These examples point to the ways in which individuals engage in harmful practices of consumption, sacrificing their health and wellbeing and going to extreme lengths in their attempts to chase and conform to the latest body trends.

These harms are further driven by an increased consumer interest in products that promise to alter their physical bodies quickly and easily. Additionally, the growing privatization of the NHS and increasing challenges in accessing health and social care services has generated opportunities for criminal activity (Yar, 2008) in the supplying of such products, compounding the potential for individual and social harm to occur. In an increasingly digitized world, online pharmacies (OPs) serve as a key platform for (counterfeit) medicine supply (Lavorgna, 2014; Di Nicola et al, 2015; Hall and Antonopoulos, 2019). Through a Google search of OPs in the UK, the results identified many illegal OPs selling large quantities of medicinal products for cosmetic purposes. To circumvent the legal restrictions and requirements in the selling of these products such sites will often be based overseas while masquerading as being based within the UK (Hall and Antonopoulos, 2016). On these sites, consumers are able to acquire 'POMs [prescription-only medicines] without a prescription ... [and access] forged online prescription services which simply ask the customer to "virtually discuss" their supposed health concerns with someone posing as an online doctor' (Hall and Antonopoulos, 2016: 34). Most OPs identified sold a range of enhancement drugs, including treatments for hair loss and weight loss, alongside a range of life-saving medicines. As such, the development of online prescription services has created opportunities for illicit parallel traders to supply products 'with less risk and also higher profit margins as it offers the consumer both convenience and choice in the market' (Hall and Antonopoulos, 2016: 30–31).

Although there are countless types of OPs supplying the UK, the distinction between legitimate and illegitimate operations is often blurred. This is because the legitimacy of a product being traded is 'spatially contingent on various regulatory frameworks in the global commodity chain' (Demant et al, 2020: 37). When examining the circulation of such goods it is imperative to consider the interplay of national and regional jurisdictional boundaries and legal systems, as unlicensed and unregulated products in one country may well be readily available elsewhere. Subsequently, if the website is trading in the UK, then they are illegally selling the product, but if it is an international website trading in the UK, their own jurisdictions may still adhere to national laws. The global reach of the web means distinguishing the legal status of operations and products being traded is complex as categories overlap, raising many questions about the legitimacy of products and transactions (Montoya and Jano, 2007). Indeed, as legal change often lags behind technological change, we are left with legislative gaps that impede the capacity for legal systems to properly operate on new and emerging spaces.

A further example of the broader trend in consumers self-managing their healthcare and beauty regimes can be seen in Hall et al's (2017) work on lifestyle drugs. They found that within UK bodybuilding subcultures there is a clear and significant 'demand for steroids and various appetite suppressants and supplements' (Hall et al, 2017: 302) with such demands often being fulfilled through counterfeit marketplaces. Additionally, through their ethnographic research, Antonopoulos and Hall (2016), Kotzé and Antonopoulos (2019) and Gibbs (2023) all identified various individual, social and economic motivations contributing to regular steroid use. Such use, they argue, is partially driven by contemporary socio-economic insecurity and marketization that generates and exacerbates anxieties around body image as well as the commodification of a muscular body (Antonopoulos and Hall, 2016). Gimlin (2002) further exemplified this and found that individuals that engage with these practices believe they are required to make 'lifestyle' choices, such as cosmetic surgery, to increase their quality of life. Despite warnings about the consequences of performance and image enhancing drugs (PIEDs) and cosmetics there is a growing trade in counterfeit lifestyle drugs in the UK (Hall and Antonopoulos, 2016; Gibbs, 2023). Thus, alongside individuals self-managing their own regimes (Hall and Antonopoulos, 2016), the shift towards privatized and individualized healthcare in the UK has emerged as a contributing factor in the demand for illicit medicines (Hall et al, 2017).

Body modification

In addition to individuals taking a more active role in their own lifestyle and healthcare regimes, body modification practices have become increasingly prevalent. The desirability of obtaining a bronzed or tanned complexion has been a relatively recent development within a Western culture that historically has emphasized a pallid complexion as exemplifying beauty. Such a view shifted in the early decades of the twentieth century when being tanned became associated with affluence and the ability to travel and go on holidays (Hunt et al, 2012). As a result, tanning through natural and unnatural methods has become an increasingly popular activity in society, despite the well-known risks. Traditional methods include outdoor sunbathing as well as the use of indoor sunbeds and sunlamps that mimic the effects of sunlight on the skin. Advancements in tanning methods such as 'fake tan' lotions and sprays, however, offer a safer way to achieve tanned skin without exposure to harmful levels of ultraviolet (UV) radiation and its associated risk to consumers, including the accelerated ageing of the skin and skin cancer. The trade in these types of products, including modern-day versions of skin whitening products, has grown considerably over the last few decades. Such growth has unsurprisingly been accompanied with a rise in the suspected counterfeiting of these products (Davey, 2016). Alternative forms of tanning methods can include the use of melanotan[1] tanning injections and nasal sprays that can produce a pigment called melanin in the skin, which can accelerate tanning. Much of the harms related to tanning injections are associated with the consumption of unregulated products sourced online by consumers (see Brennan et al, 2014).

Contrastingly, within Black and Asian communities there are cultural preferences and practices that attempt to achieve a lighter complexion due to associated beliefs that such a complexion is representative of beauty, health and wealth (Smit et al, 2009). As a result, some individuals with darker skin tones attempt to achieve a lighter skin tone through the use of skin whitening products (Pollock et al, 2021). Skin bleaching and lightening products aim to lighten dark areas of skin or achieve a generally lighter skin tone and complexion. These products can contain highly toxic active ingredients and are typically designed for medical and cosmetic purposes that aim to decrease the level of melanin in the skin. Physical harm associated with 'under the counter' bleaching agents such as skin blistering and kidney problems have made the use of these products a health concern for Black and Asian communities around the world (Tate, 2017).

Another form of body modification that has become increasingly popular in Western culture is the wearing of tattoos. Tattooing has a long and well-documented history (Sanders and Vail, 2008) and is appropriately regulated in the UK, making it a relatively safe practice. Nevertheless, the increasing popularity and demand for tattoos has been accompanied by a rise in 'backstreet tattooing', which poses significant risks to public health and safety as it is often delivered by unlicensed tattooists operating without appropriate qualifications or training, using substandard equipment and products in unsterilized studios. Not only does this put individuals at risk of getting a poor-quality tattoo, but it can also potentially cause significant physical harm through allergic reactions, as well as through an increased risk of infections such as hepatitis and HIV (see Campbell, 2019a). Similarly, Henna tattooing has been around for thousands of years and remains a popular practice among some communities. Henna 'ink' comes from all-natural ingredients, and it is a relatively safe practice that is not permanent. However, the use of black henna, which contains the chemical ingredient para-phenylenediamine, can cause physical harm such chemical burns, blistering and scarring (see Ritschel, 2018).

Despite fashion trends and ideals evolving and adapting over time, the negative effects and consequences accompanying consumer practices and products remain ever-present. Consequently, the willingness to impose harm on the self, on others, and on the environment is not an epiphenomenon of the contemporary production and supply of beauty. From a social harm perspective, Large (2019: 64) argues that 'although consumers are sold ideals of free choice and identity expression through fashion, the reality is that the nature of fashion is one which is structurally and systemically harmful'. The growing demand to consume, driven by the persistent trend cycle, causes a desire for immediate emotional gratification. This stems from the social structures of late capitalism and subjectivities embedded in consumer culture, which are characterized by anxiety, insecurities, precarity (Hall et al, 2008; Lloyd, 2013) and unsustainable levels of consumer debt (Davis and Cartwright, 2019). Such social conditions give fertile ground to the circulation of counterfeit and illegitimate products that provide indebted and precarious individuals a means to consume that which would otherwise be unobtainable (see Chapter 5). The presence of illegally produced and sold products alongside legal products that are illegally sold (for example, stolen goods), creates a grey area in the trade industry. As such, it is important to consider both the legal and illegal aspects of the industry in parallel to fully examine the ways in which social harms circulate.

The legal and illegal markets

Given the rapid growth of e-commerce, legitimate and illegitimate businesses are in constant competition to capture the time, attention and money of consumers. Illicit and licit markets tend to be understood by many law enforcement agencies and officials as being two entirely different markets (OECD, 2008). However, the reality is that the consumption of counterfeit goods does not differ much from usual consumer behaviour (Large, 2019). The demand for cheap branded products to display consumer symbolism is constituted and reproduced through late-modern consumer culture (Hall et al, 2008). Rutter and Bryce (2008) argue that the purchasing of counterfeit goods is strongly associated with everyday routines, people and places, rather than being the domain of criminal acts associated with subcultures and stigma. For them, the consumption of counterfeit goods mirrors the demand and consumption of legal goods and is often a means for consumers to better manage their spending across the marketplace of available products. The sustainability of illicit and illegal markets is fundamentally reliant on the consumption of products more generally (Large, 2018).

Similarly, there has been limited consideration of the ways in which the legitimate fashion marketplaces and trends can spur consumers into purchasing and engaging with counterfeited version of branded products (Juggesur and Cohen, 2009: 384). Indeed, it is suggested that the issue of counterfeiting is, in part, rooted in the industry itself (Hilton et al, 2004). For example, Large's (2019) research on consumer perspectives of counterfeiting shows that although consumers held a strong concern about the manufacturing and production of counterfeits, this was also the case for the manufacturing and producing of fashion goods more generally. Such issues are also present within the beauty industry, where fashion and trends are a significant factor as businesses constantly vie for market share and popularity as they compete. Similarly, the beauty industry, along with other consumer industries (for example, the health and fitness industries), features extensive imitation to keep in line with trends, cycles and fads. Certain aspects of copying tend to be allowed because 'the desire for free and full competition outweighs concerns about imitation' (Raustiala and Sprigman, 2012: 170). As such, the illicit and licit are entangled: one would not exist without the other and it is necessary to critically consider the legal parallel market when examining illicit markets (Large, 2018). Additionally, Hobbs (2012: 265) highlights the importance of looking at the rise of the market society and suggests that we should not be blind to 'the attractions of market behaviour that makes nonsense of the often arbitrary distinctions between legal and illegal business'. By fixating on the criminal aspects of counterfeiting the importance of understanding the wider demands of global trade are missed. This aspect of an ineffable distinction from the illicit markets can be seen in numerous studies (Tom et al, 1998; Wilcox et al, 2009; Bian et al, 2016), all of which fail to interrogate the underlying drives, motivations and desires of consumption more generally. While it is often an analytical necessity to separate the licit and illicit markets to better understand the size, scope and practices inherent in illicit markets, such a move is a misstep that serves to conceal or minimize the real and legitimate ways in which harms are created and perpetuated by the licit marketplace.

The growing demand for cheap and quick products is having detrimental effects on the world, with the phenomenon of 'shoppers seeking something new to wear every week' creating a constant cycle of consumers purchasing and disposing of products. Younger consumers appear to be particularly unaware of the environmental consequences and harms caused by their habits (Morgan and Birtwistle, 2009: 190). The relationship between the fashion and beauty industry and environmental degradation is an issue that demands further attention (Large, 2019). The United Nations (2019) claims that the fashion industry has become 'the second most polluting industry in the world'. At the same time, public concern has grown around the poor procedures and practices of fashion and beauty companies, leading to increased exposure of a range of ethical issues in the international supply chain of fashion and beauty including the use of child labour, exploitation, poor working conditions, environmental degradation, unsustainable production and animal welfare. Post-consumption waste is a significant challenge in the world of fashion, and one that has no easy fixes (Ecowatch, 2023; Wrap, 2023).

Similarly, the beauty industry has also been responsible for a great deal of waste that has taken a toll on the environment, with the use of single-use plastics and microbeads in cosmetic products (see UNEP, 2015). The beauty and fashion industries have attempted to respond to such environmental harms for some time; however, the reuse and end-of-use management issues have only recently been considered (for example, the shift from single-use cotton-wool pads to reusable pads). Thus, as Ferrell (2006) identified in the *Empire of Scrounge* and Smith and Raymen (2018: 72) have advocated more recently: 'the environmental harms associated with waste produced by a globalised consumer culture is only going to intensify over time as the demands of a consumer economy and its neophiliac subjects consume and discard fashions, fads and trends in an ever-shortening life cycle of commodities.'

Hvass (2015) identified two main strategies that fashion companies are using to control the post-retail phase of their products: product take-back schemes and resell/reuse platforms. Similar schemes have started to emerge in the beauty industry, with beauty recycling schemes launching in physical and online stores.[2] However, due to the nature of beauty products, post-consumption initiatives are limited.

The waste and pollution generated at all stages of the supply chain, particularly through the consumption of energy and the transportation requirements of both raw materials and manufactured goods, are also of great concern (Large, 2018: 236). Consequently, the high turnover rate associated with production in the fashion industry has huge consequences for the wider environment, and problems related to harmful waste disposal practices, regardless of their legality, are a growing problem. This problem is exacerbated when considering the clear crossover with fashion and beauty, with the ongoing demand for cheap beauty products and services such as cosmetics, skin products, makeovers, weight-loss products and electricals such as hair styling and hair removal tools. In addition, with the rise of social media influencers producing shopping 'haul videos', the excess of plastic packaging and unwanted products being sent to influencers is widespread (Rigby, 2019). Sophie, for example, was a social media influencer and told me about how she often receives beauty products that she did not ask for, nor want:

> It's nice to receive free gifts but sometimes there is so much waste. You get a massive box delivered and inside is something tiny surrounded by an unnecessary amount of packaging. Half the time the products aren't really things I want or need. I got sent some beauty brushes last month, but that's the third time I've had brushes sent to me. I don't need that many, it's such a waste. It's hardly surprising the big-time influencers are doing hauls and de-clutter videos all the time.

Thus, alongside the fashion industry, the beauty industry contributes to this mass disposal attitude and is likely to be as problematic in relation to the wider view of environmental harm.

A further issue with the beauty industry is the poor production practices that are often linked to unsafe working conditions. For example, it has been reported that some supply chains for luxury perfume brands may encourage the 'worst form of child labour', using minors to pick jasmine and other ingredients (see ElShamy and Cox, 2024). Additionally, mica, an ingredient that is used in many cosmetic products, has captured the attention of the British public after the use of child labour in mica mining came to light (Irvine, 2017). According to a report from SOMO (2016: 7–8) around 90 per cent of mica mining is illegal, and the number of child labourers involved in mica mining in the states of Jharkhand and Bihar in India is estimated to be up to 20,000. Despite this scrutiny, some cosmetic manufacturers continue to source and use mica in their products. There are some attempts within the industry to combat such practices, for example, the 'responsible mica initiative' is a global cross-industry collaboration working to eradicate child labour and poor working conditions within the Indian mica supply chain (see Responsible Mica Initiative, 2018). These are just some examples of the working conditions in the global beauty industry.

Also relevant when considering the harms associated with the beauty industry is animal testing. Cosmetic industries have always faced criticism for testing products on animals. In 2013, the EU banned the sale of cosmetics (and their ingredients) developed through animal testing, making it illegal to sell cosmetic products that have been tested on animals (Rowser, 2020).

While this discussion surrounding harm has shifted to a focus on the legitimate industry, all of these issues are equally applicable to the mirroring counterfeit beauty industry. For example, counterfeit cosmetic products may have been tested on animals or caused harm to animals due to the lack of regulation. In addition, laboratory tests on counterfeit beauty goods have revealed the presence of a range of poisonous chemicals, toxic levels of chemicals, and even human urine and rat droppings (see IPO, 2024), all of which can cause temporary and longer-term health problems. As this section has demonstrated, it is critically important to consider both the illicit market and the parallel legal market to fully understand the breadth of the complexities, drivers and harms of the counterfeit beauty industry (Hall and Antonopoulos, 2016; Large, 2018).

Harmful trends and unrealistic beauty standards

Globalization has transformed the ways in which fashion and beauty trends are transmitted and circulated. Prior to globalization, the upper class had greater access to wealth and leisure time, allowing them to dictate fashion trends which were then vertically transmitted to the middle and lower classes to imitate. Although these individuals would not be able to afford the same materials, they would emulate the general styles using cheaper materials and less complex designs. Trends in fashion have become more readily available to consumers all over the world. Access to images has evolved significantly, from limited exposure to widespread dissemination of photographs and media sources more generally in contemporary society.

With the influx of visual imagery through mass media, technologies can reproduce ideologies of how women should look by using idealized images of 'beautiful' women (Wolf, 2002). Men's interest in beauty has also seen a rise in recent years as gender norms are morphing and masculinity ideals are shifting (Bryne and Milestone, 2023). With beauty being important for both women and men, it is becoming increasingly unrealistic to attain the minimum expected beauty standards, as ideas of what it means to be 'good enough' are constantly changing (Widdows, 2018). As Widdows (2018: 127) infers, 'technology has exponentially extended the possibilities of what we can do in seeking to be normal, better, or perfect'. This extension of the beauty ideal leads individuals to meet the demands placed upon them through engaging with affordable and available products and procedures, despite the inherent dangers, risks and possible harms associated with bodily and facial enhancement. Consequently, the contemporary beauty market is shaped by a combination of technological change, the rise of digital consumerism, and shifting ideals and expectations of gendered norms of femininity and masculinity.

The proliferation of more traditional forms of media throughout the twentieth and twenty-first centuries, including magazines, television and advertisements, paved the way for the transmission and consumption of unrealistic beauty standards that have driven industry sales. Numerous studies and reports have illustrated considerable evidence for the effects and influences of media on body image, self-perfection and body dissatisfaction (Bell and Dittmar, 2011; Yar, 2012; Cashmore, 2023). An example of this form of media exposure can be seen in Protein World's controversial weight-loss advertisement in 2015, causing many individuals to feel physically inferior to the unrealistic 'idealized' body that was displayed and the headline of 'Are you beach body ready?' (see Hackman, 2015). The lack of boundaries in the marketing of products for the 'perfect' body is therefore causing individuals to feel a sense of inadequacy, and a need to consume these products and/or services to obtain this 'idealized' body image. Within media content such as magazines, television programmes and advertisements that focus on body image, a surveillance lens detecting flaws and scrutinizing the bodies of others has become more intense. One clear example of this is often found in magazines with the use of 'close-ups, magnification, red circles and highlighted areas (e.g. to draw attention to cellulite or an un-depilated hair or other aesthetic "transgressions")' (Elias et al, 2017: 14).

Social media and digital platforms

The rise of social media platforms in the twenty-first century has provided 'another space and opportunity for the competitive and comparative display of lifestyle, cultural and consumer competence' (Smith and Raymen, 2018: 11). Online spaces allow consumers to present the 'networked self' (Quinn and Papacharissi, 2018) and share accomplishments and display economic success, consumer lifestyles and consumption practices in real-time. The constant sharing has caused peer surveillance to become an increasingly common part of life, where individuals from various social institutions – friends, family, employers and educators – now monitor the display and actions of others (Abidin, 2016; Diefenbach and Christoforakos, 2017; Duffy and Chan, 2019). In respect to Veblen (2005) and Mestrovic (2003), individualization is achieved through the means of self-aggrandizement. The need to portray oneself in a way that encourages a sense of envy and admiration in the other is becoming standard practice within contemporary society. On social media, selectively deciding what images or text to upload for others to view is common among individuals attempting to display their lifestyles to others and gain social recognition and external validation. This kind of 'will to represent' (Yar, 2012: 252) through the process of taking, posting and viewing selfies has become a daily habit for many (Diefenbach and Christoforakos, 2017).

As such, the internet 'gives users a freedom of expression – a freedom of being – quite unlike anything they have at their disposal in the physical world' (Jewkes and Sharp, 2003: 2). However, this freedom is superficial. Consumer capitalism cultivates an intermittent sense of dissatisfaction of what one has to ultimately create this sense of need and desire to uphold the ever-shortening lifecycle of commodities and the 'velocity of fashion' (Appadurai, 1986; Baudrillard, 1998). As cultural criminologists such as Hayward (2004: 161) stipulate, individuals tend to have a 'constant sense of unfulfillment' as consumption has shifted to being 'fundamentally expected' and a 'basic right', rather than something that is 'culturally desirable'.

The use of post-production processes (for example, the use of filters) following the capture of an image has become an integral aspect, and for many a fundamental component, of their engagement with social media and online spaces. It is now a common practice to pose and take images of oneself to post on a social media site (Diefenbach and Christoforakos, 2017). Technological advances enable young people to not only upload images onto social media sites with ease but to modify these images using computer and smartphone apps. There are thousands of appearance and beauty apps available such as Instaglam, Modiface, Beauty Mirror and AEDIT: AI Plastic Surgeon, alongside more traditional digital tools such as Photoshop. These apps enable users to erase flaws and enhance appearances through digital makeovers, facelifts, face and body slimming, new hair styles, lip enhancements and other functions that allow users to alter their appearance and 'try on' new aesthetic trends and cosmetic procedures. However, as Elias and Gill (2017: 10) argue, beauty apps 'increase the extent to which the female body and face are rendered visible as a site of crisis and commodification'. This is not just the case for women, as there is an increase in similar apps aimed specifically at men. For example, the Manly app, a photo editor for men that allows the user to add toned 'abs' (abdominal muscles) to the body and 'be the manly version of yourself'.

The use of such apps is inescapable for many, as Jones (2012: 194) argues, 'the most fashionable faces are now the most visibly manufactured: they are the faces that are created and presented with the aids of lightening, photography, makeup, computer software, pharmacology and surgery'. Social media has played a role in plastic surgery practices, with plastic surgeons utilizing this new avenue of communication (see Wheeler et al, 2011). The capabilities offered by computerized and mobile technologies are shifting the way we experience our embodied selves and the way that we relate to one another (Elias and Gill, 2017). Unattainable images of beauty were once a figment of the imagination, but modification apps and software have enabled unrealistic images of perfection to become a tangible reality. As such, the Western enthusiasm for a desired body type and the elusive 'ideal' body image, influenced by celebrities and those with high social standing, play a large role in society's general feelings of inadequacy (Russell-Mayhew et al, 2022; Cashmore, 2023). Therefore, this upsurge in computerized apps to enhance physical appearance can arguably exacerbate dissatisfaction with the self, unearthing further anxieties that can be detrimental to mental health.

This raises the concern that self-modification apps and technological filters are intimately shaping the cultural dissatisfaction of one's body image through feelings of shame and failure, which can ultimately lead to oneself undertaking harmful beauty practices to achieve the desired look full-time (see Hughes, 2017). The intensification of beauty pressures is targetting all ages, with media, cosmetics and fashion being drilled into younger age groups with magazines such as *Teen Vogue* promoting the perfect complexion and exposing young people to the ideal look through images of celebrities. The presentation of idealized body images, the internet and social media platforms have increasingly become trusted sources for beauty, health and wellbeing information for all ages and genders. The virtual environment has become a central hub for individuals seeking tips on 'DIY' beauty and weight loss (Wood, 2024). The pressure to have pixel-perfect skin is of particular harm to consumers, where there is a rise in the number of individuals using unsuitable beauty products and injecting potentially harmful amounts of Botox and dermal filler into their faces in attempts to enhance their appearance. Anti-ageing measures are being taken earlier than ever, where youth is being extended before it has even finished and faces that are still developing and maturing are being injected with enhancement drugs. For example, a rising trend on TikTok is the influencing of young children to use skincare products designed for adults, posing a potential risk of irreversible skin damage (see Rackham, 2024). Additionally, individuals are now able to learn how to self-inject through online YouTube videos, which are typically recommended in online forums (Brennan et al, 2019). As will be examined in Chapter 6, the beauty industry is increasingly marketing more products to a younger demographic and, coupled with the ease of acquiring knowledge and products, is leading to the potential for a growing number of young people enlisting in a lifetime of beauty maintenance (Berkowitz, 2017).

The hyper-connectedness of selling and consuming beauty in virtual and physical spaces

Rapidly advancing digital technologies are 'probing and perforating the boundaries between [suppliers] and consumers, production and consumption, object and image', and the physical and the virtual (Crewe, 2017: 10). The spatial flexibilization of consuming and supplying beauty has had profound effects on the nature of beauty practices more generally, and risk-laden beauty practices in particular. For example, anyone from any location can now go onto the internet to buy weight-loss drugs and cosmetic enhancement products. And, just like one of the participants, Carys, they can use YouTube and online forums to learn how to use and administer the products. As such, the use and supply of (illicit) beauty products and services appears to be legitimized and normalized through their relationship with other forms of leisure such as fitness activities, the night-time economy (NTE) and online social networks. The expanding non-stop processes of twenty-first-century capitalism has, thus, almost entirely blurred boundaries between the various spheres of public and private life, work and social life, and leisure and consumption (Crary, 2013). The hyper-connectedness between these spheres undeniably shapes the demand for, and supply and consumption of, beauty and counterfeit beauty. This has therefore changed both contemporary selling and the role of beauty and beauty ideals in late capitalism.

The shopping experience is no longer restricted to traditional business hours or physical locations. The 24/7 functioning of capitalism has facilitated the marketplace to operate every hour of the day, across different time zones and geographical boundaries, allowing the contemporary subject to shop and communicate anywhere and at any time. Although the internet offers a certain degree of anonymity to users, it also extends opportunities for sellers and consumers, and consumers and other consumers to build relationships, exchange personal experiences and knowledge, and recommend certain products and sellers. The participatory and active roles consumers now take in these online spaces of consumption can enable the distribution of knowledge and coerce individuals into purchasing illicit products from certain online sellers. The networked and digital affordances associated with social media have widened opportunities for individuals to create, share and respond to content, and earn money through a greater range of channels at faster speeds. This has led to some shifts in not just the extent but also the nature of consumption and supply. For example, with the rise of user-generated content, such as blogs and even 'review' sections of retailer websites (for example, Asos or Look Fantastic), the balance of power between consumers and producers in terms of who shapes brand perception and who becomes the beauty expert has blurred. Virtual relationships are now commonly formed on social media and in forums, where customers, potential customers and sellers can collectively discuss their experiences with products, knowledge of products and experiences with suppliers. The following excerpt illustrates a discussion between two 'consumers' in a forum related to weight loss:

User 1: I bought Reductil online. I saw a Facebook page for buying Reductil and Sibutramine and read through the comments. There are still a couple of places you can get it from without a prescription. The bad news is that it's pretty expensive. The cheapest I've found it for is £105 for 20 tablets (1 per day). Has anyone found it cheaper? Here is the link …

User 2: The link doesn't work. I think the website has shut down. I can't seem to find Reductil anywhere. I've switched over to use Xenical. 120mg x 60 pills for £102. They have an offer at the moment and it's only £80! You don't need a prescription. Message me if you are interested and I'll send you the website details.

User 1: Cheers mate. I've messaged you – looking forward to giving them a go.

These types of discussions were common in online spaces associated with beauty, fitness and health, where consumers voluntarily shared experiences and opinions on certain products, avenues to purchase them and how much they paid for them. On social media sites and within forums there was not always a clear demarcation between sellers and buyers involved in promoting and recommending products. With the development of Web 2.0, the traditional distinctions between producers and consumers have become increasingly blurred as they have been influenced by the participatory nature of social interactions in online spaces (Ritzer and Jurgenson, 2010); we are no longer passive consumers, we are all potential producers. The rise of user-generated content online has encouraged users to create profiles composed of videos, photos and text, interact with one another and build online communities.

Social media sites, forums and blogs all allow the exchange of information, where consumers can take an active role in sharing their consumption practices (Beer and Burrows, 2010). Other websites such as eBay, Etsy, YouTube, Pinterest and Tripadvisor all rely on consumers to take this active role in implicitly producing its content, where these markets are mostly made up of 'prosumers' (producer-consumers) (Beer and Burrows, 2010). This melding of consumption and production highlights a process of 'prosumption' (Beer and Burrows, 2010) emerging in counterfeit trading, 'where often there is no clear demarcation between the producer, trader and consumer involved in marketing and advertising' (Hall and Antonopoulos, 2016: 39). These 'prosumers' engage with 'appearance markets' as a means of creative self-expression and play an active role in shaping and producing beauty ideals as part of a broader and more important shift towards participatory web cultures created within user participation and user-generated content. Therefore, online participatory networks act as an avenue through which users can discuss, obtain and disseminate knowledge of illicit products, services and sellers, where a 'lack of trust, anonymity and individualism combine as … "push and pull", motivating factors' (Hall and Antonopoulos, 2016: 59) to facilitate the supply and consumption of the illicit beauty and the lifestyle drug trade.

Furthermore, the widespread use of social media platforms, digital communication tools and online communities has reshaped the contemporary digital landscape. Social media platforms play a central role in DIY cosmetic injection practices, where individuals attempt to administer cosmetic injections, often without medical training. A large quantity of Botox and dermal filler tutorials were identified through YouTube searches using the keywords 'Botox tutorial' and 'How to inject Botox and filler'. This included videos on how to mix the products, prepare syringes and inject different regions of the face with Botox and dermal filler products. Alongside some basic training provided by her supplier, the accessibility of injecting tutorials on YouTube enabled Carys to self-inject cosmetic products and provide a service for others. Carys considered YouTube as the medium through which she could access information and knowledge to 'safely' inject Botox and dermal fillers and deemed herself as an 'expert' in the industry:

> You have to be very careful not to hit a blood vessel, or you'll end up with really bad bruising or worse. I find it a lot easier to inject myself than others. I suppose that's because when you inject others, there is a whole new pressure not to fuck it up. I'm more worried about damaging someone else's face than my own. Learning to do it yourself is so much cheaper. If there hadn't been videos on YouTube, I don't think I would've had the confidence. But there are so many different videos and tips online. I spent so much time on YouTube watching [tutorials] and making sure I knew what I was doing. I think I do a better job [than the professionals].

In today's socially mediated world where anyone can upload or access and watch online injecting tutorials and emulate the observed to become a 'beauty expert', we can begin to see how YouTube, forums and social media sites have transformed the nature of the market for cosmetic enhancements and play a powerful role in shaping social practices (Brennan et al, 2019). With so much information readily available on the internet, anyone can share knowledge, experiences and position themselves as a specialist in beauty and cosmetic enhancement practices. This interconnection between the online and offline worlds is arguably reshaping the beauty industry.

Moreover, shopping practices are now thoroughly embedded in the mundanity of everyday life, including at work, while commuting, in pubs and bars, in the evenings at home while watching reality television and while laying in bed in the middle of the night. As this form of intuitive purchasing has been enabled by the use of smartphones and become spatially separated from the traditional shopping arenas, individuals in contemporary society are constantly seeking pleasure through consumption, regardless of their location or the time. This negation of space and time by the increasing speed of information flows leads to a shift towards what Castells (2010) terms as 'timeless time'. The experience of 'actual' social space has shifted from tangible locations (nightclubs, bars and so on) to immaterial social networks, in which the contemporary subject is relentlessly living through their smartphone. In addition, retailers employ various marketing techniques, such as personalized emails and push notifications, to offer convenient and quick ways to shop online. For example, 'Hey. you forgot something …' (Asos) and 'Step this way for up to 45% off everything' (MyProtein). Through a constant stream of information about the latest products and services, new promotions, personalized offers that are tailored to individual consumer preferences, and reminders to return to our abandoned baskets and complete the purchase, the contemporary subject is persistently encouraged to make unplanned purchases and spend more.

That this relentless pursuit of pleasure ultimately fails to provide an individual with any sense of fulfilment is a display of what Mark Fisher (2009) refers to as 'depressive hedonia'. Fisher (2009) argues that this is not the typical anhedonia that we commonly link with depression, rather it is the 'inability to do anything else except pursue pleasure' (Fisher, 2009: 22). There is a pervasive feeling that 'something is missing', yet there is no appreciation that this missing sense of enjoyment lies 'beyond the pleasure principle' (Fisher, 2009: 22). The young people I spoke with were in a perpetual state of restlessness, browsing online shopping sites at any given moment, engaging in endless cycles of purchasing and returning items, and compulsively checking social media for fashion trends and updates. In fact, the panic of not checking and responding to e-mails and messages or checking social media is pervasive within the context of late capitalism (Crary, 2013).

As increasingly more time is being spent online, the physical and virtual worlds are converging, and we can no longer distinguish between the two realities: offline does not exist without online. For example, within physical spaces for fitness, such as gyms, individuals and communities come together to support each other in achieving their common goals (for example, losing body fat, gaining muscle) in ways that go beyond the physical gym environment. The contemporary subject does not just attend the gym, they also virtually document their physical transformations and workouts on social media, discuss their exercise and diet regimes within fitness-related Facebook groups and follow workouts and obtain nutrition tips from the latest social media influencers. As Lister et al (2009: 217) suggest, 'cyberspace … is not more separate from the material world than any other kind of mediated experience and indeed precisely because of its ubiquity may in fact be more seamlessly and intimately stitched into everyday life'. We now live in a hyperreality, where stimulations of reality appear more real than reality itself (Baudrillard, 1983).

Recognizing the hyper-connectedness of online and offline, and the consumer and the supplier, is central to understanding contemporary forms of harm, not only because of the material opportunities it provide, but also because of the way they profoundly reshape human experience and subjectivity. The context of 'real' life itself is not something separate from the virtual world, but rather it works in tandem as the internet enables individuals to always be connected to consumer communities. Therefore, it is crucial that when conceptualizing beauty harms, we move beyond digital dualist arguments that position the online and offline as separate and disconnected spheres (Jurgenson, 2012) and instead examine how the online and offline have become enmeshed (Crewe, 2017) within contemporary beauty practices and consumption in Western culture. In this regard the consumption of potentially harmful products and information online is extending into physical harms offline, and there is a danger that by separating the two spheres the harms experienced online become marginalized and minimized (Gosse, 2021).

Chapter summary

This chapter has examined the history of fashion trends, the pursuit of ever-changing beauty ideals and how these have contributed to the normalization, acceptance and celebration of harmful practices throughout history. Individuals have always gone to extreme lengths to conform to the beauty standards and expectations of the time, and technological developments have amplified harmful consumer practices in the fashion and beauty industries within contemporary society. Consumer motivations for beauty function across gender boundaries and are often grounded in common subjective feelings of inferiority and dissatisfaction that consumer capitalism intensifies, exploits and thrives upon.

The latter part of this chapter has introduced the reader to the hyper-connectedness of the online and offline and the ways in which this has fundamentally altered the consumption of beauty products and services. This chapter has ultimately served to demonstrate how the contemporary beauty industry creates and encourages a growing population of young people to engage with it despite the associated harms.

4

The Contemporary Seller and the Myth of the 'Organized Criminal'

Introduction

Following discussions in Chapter 2 of the paradigmatic explanatory frameworks for selling counterfeits, this chapter examines the supply-side of the online and localized offline market in Beaufort. This includes offline distribution avenues to online sellers, and the role of the internet in the local trade of beauty counterfeits. The offline distribution networks, the gym and the salon, are explored using observations and participant accounts of their legitimate and illicit working practices and the skills required for both. The online environment of illicit supply will then be unpacked, including how offline sellers procure stock from online sources, use social media platforms to learn how to 'safely' inject cosmetic enhancements and the role of the internet in selling and advertising illicit beauty products and services. The final section brings the first two sections together to address how backgrounds and experiences shape young people's willingness to engage in selling practices, and their positions as consumers focused on improving their identity and appearance. This chapter advances the argument that these young people's selling practices do not fit into many of the traditional explanatory frameworks for selling counterfeits, which tend to dominate criminology's theoretical repertoire.

The offline beauty marketplace

The intertwinement of licit and illicit business

Common assumptions associated with the supplying of counterfeits maintain that the sale of counterfeits is linked to organized criminal enterprise such as trafficking, terrorist funding, sexual exploitation and violent activities

(Naylor, 2002; Lowe, 2006; Home Office, 2022). However, the structure of illicit beauty distribution networks is usually woven into the fabric of conventional routine (Hall and Antonopoulos, 2015; van de Ven and Mulrooney, 2017), as was the case in Beaufort where four offline sellers engaged in illicit opportunities arising from their legitimate occupations. These legitimate activities provided offline sellers with a steady income, a pre-existing clientele and a 'cover' for their illicit operation. Such operations involved the sale of counterfeit and illicit items alongside legitimate products. They used legal channels to distribute illicit beauty products and services that would have otherwise not met safety or regulatory standards. Before unpacking the structure of the distribution networks, however, two key offline sites that I observed and interacted with – Radiance and EvolveGym – are introduced.

Introducing the tanning salon

> It was good fortune and mutual friends that brought me into the company of Lauren, the manager of Radiance, an independent tanning salon. Arriving at a bar in Beaufort on a Saturday night to celebrate a friend's birthday, I made my way through a crowd of stylish individuals in their late twenties, and spotted a group with some familiar faces huddled together and clinking glasses in celebration of Megan's birthday. Glamorously dressed, each person exuded confidence as they shared stories and swayed to the rhythm of the music. A few of us made superficial conversation for several minutes, before being directed to a reserved seating area where a mutual friend started introducing us all to one another. The first person I encountered was Lauren, 27 years old, and of average height. She embodied the look of other women in Beaufort: false eyelashes, a glowing tan, manicured nails, white teeth and bouncy blow-dried hair extensions. It did not take long during our first meeting for her to be enthused over her work. As a salon manager, Lauren had a lot to say about her role and how the upsurge of other beauty businesses had impacted the site she manages, along with the various tanning methods that are available today. Lauren's position and eagerness to talk about her work made it clear that she would be a tremendous source of information for this research.
>
> The following week Lauren invited me to the salon for a coffee. The salon was relatively small and had a crushed velvet interior, which was a standard feature of many beauty salons in the area. On the reception desk, there was a small display of branded tanning lotions in sachets and bottles. The salon had four different sunbed rooms to choose from, and the stand-up sunbed had a 'built-in vibration plate' so customers could 'tone the body while having a sunbed'. As we sat on the sofa adjacent to the reception

> desk, I noticed multiple brown boxes stacked up behind the desk. On the front of one of the boxes in black marker pen, it said: 'Tanning Lotions 2'. I later found out these were counterfeits. (fieldnote)

Lauren had worked in the salon for eight years, six of which she had been a manager and three she had been selling illicit goods. Leveraging her professional position and experience, Lauren had purchased a range of counterfeit tanning lotions and melanotan II (M2) tanning injections and nasal sprays online to sell in the salon in order to supplement her legitimate income that she deemed insufficient. She was also a consumer of various counterfeit and non-counterfeit make-up products and clothing items and purchased these through social media platforms. She admitted she had never tried the tanning lotions, but frequently used the M2 injections and nasal sprays. The following section offers a similar opportune encounter with a personal trainer (PT) at a local gym, further highlighting the significance of offline legitimate businesses and peer networks to sell illicit beauty.

Introducing the gym

Early in my offline fieldwork, I joined EvolveGym, a gym in Beaufort, and frequented it most mornings. Through this I initiated contact with other members and also staff, such as Brandon (21), a self-employed PT in the gym. Although I already knew Brandon from my previous membership with EvolveGym, I was unaware of his illicit selling activities until around six months into the fieldwork, when I was in the right place at the right time.

> It was a Friday morning and I entered EvolveGym. As I walked through the doors, my attention was immediately drawn to Brandon sitting in the café area, scrolling through his phone with a coffee in hand. Brandon had worked at the gym for over two years, and before working there he regularly frequented it as a member. Not only did Brandon work long days, but he also spent a lot of his leisure time training at EvolveGym. Around six-feet tall with a muscular physique, Brandon exuded confidence and an element of intimidation, but as soon as he spoke he was instantly disarming due to his friendly manner. It was clear he was not there to train or work; he was wearing jeans and a hoodie. We talked for a short time, as we would most mornings, and he told me he was waiting to meet someone. One of the other morning regulars, Cal, walked into the gym and Brandon handed him a small brown package in exchange for some money. Cal quickly disappeared to the changing rooms. Without thinking much of it, Brandon and I continued to chat as normal. Five minutes later another person walked into the gym to see Brandon. She slipped Brandon some money

> in exchange for a slightly larger package and sat on the chair next to him. They both seemed uncomfortable, and the atmosphere was unwelcoming. At this point, I left to exercise.
>
> Throughout my workout I kept thinking about the exchanges I had witnessed; should I have asked what he was selling? After about thirty minutes I decided to go and see if Brandon was still there. I quickly downed the rest of my water and entered the café without appearing intrusive or suspicious. Brandon was sitting in the same spot, scrolling Facebook on his phone. He looked up and asked me how my workout was going. We proceeded to talk about fitness and the conversation effortlessly led back to Cal. I sat and listened to Brandon for around an hour as he spoke about how he sold 'fake' products. During our lengthy conversation, three other customers came to see Brandon, and this was all before 7.30 am. It transpired that alongside owning a reasonably successful PT business, Brandon sold M2 tanning injections and a range of counterfeit perfumes and aftershaves to gym members and close friends outside of the gym. He explained that he had only recently started selling M2 products but had been selling counterfeit fragrances since his teens. (fieldnote)

Similar to Lauren, Brandon's operation used legal channels to distribute illicit beauty products and services. Such selling practices do not fit into many of the conventional explanatory frameworks for selling counterfeits that often dominate the theoretical landscape, and this blurring and blending of legitimate and illegitimate labour activities are found in offline and online settings.

Procuring stock for local trade

Online markets played an important role in the local trade of illicit beauty in Beaufort. Lauren sold M2 tanning injections and nasal sprays sourced through an Ireland-based website and Brandon sold M2 tanning injections sourced from 'somewhere in the UK'. A Google search for 'tanning injections UK' returned approximately eight websites selling M2 products. Most claimed to be UK-based, with the products on sale being listed for research purposes only. This was outlined in the 'terms and conditions' section of one website:

> IMPORTANT Website content:
>
> Articles, information and videos provided on website are strictly for INFORMATION ONLY, they should not be read or taken as a guide on how to use any product purchased on this site. Products are sold for RESEARCH PURPOSES ONLY AND NOT TO BE USED FOR TANNING OR SLIMMING PURPOSES. If the buyer uses for these purposes the Seller can not be held liable in any form.

> Use of Products:
>
> The Suppliers products are intended for research purposes and are not to be used for any other purpose, including but not limited to, in vitro diagnostic purposes, in foods, drugs, medical devices, or cosmetics for humans or animals or for commercial purposes. The Buyer acknowledges that the products have not been tested by supplier for safety and efficacy in food, drug, and medical device, cosmetic, commercial or any other use. The Buyer expressly represents and warrants to supplier that the Buyer will properly test, use, manufacture and market any products purchased from supplier and/or materials produced with products purchased from supplier in accordance with the practices of reasonable person who is an expert in the field and in strict compliance with all applicable laws and regulations, now and hereinafter enacted.

Furthermore, some websites had sections offering guidance on how to use tanning injections, advising customers to use them alongside sunbeds to get 'maximum results', and marketing the products as a way to achieve a 'deep long-lasting tan'. While these websites claimed that the information provided was for 'research purposes only', they were arguably attempting to bypass laws, as the products are unlicensed for cosmetic use and have not been tested for safety by the Medicines and Healthcare products Regulatory Agency (MHRA). These products were available for anyone to purchase at a click of a button, without providing proof that the products would be used for research purposes only.

As mentioned in Chapter 3, this circumvention of existing regulations has created opportunities for websites to operate and distribute M2 products to consumers for cosmetic use. Brown (2006) has highlighted that conventional law has difficulty operating in digital spaces. Similarly, less regulated websites and 'zones of ambiguity' (Hornsby and Hobbs, 2007) have long been attractive to opportunistic criminal entrepreneurs as they provide a space where illegal trading can easily take place (Treadwell, 2011). Therefore, products at the margins of legitimacy provided the research participants with an easy avenue for procuring and selling stock in offline settings. Although Lauren and Brandon were aware of the illicit nature of these products, such websites can potentially mislead consumers into believing the products on sale are authentic, licensed and safe.

The management and interpretation of risk in the offline beauty marketplace

Given the illegitimate nature of the offline participants' activities, many were well versed in risk management. They meticulously described the ways they encountered and navigated the risk of incurring official and unofficial repercussions for their involvement in selling illicit goods. Lauren, for example, demonstrated an awareness that she was undertaking a substantial risk and looked to mitigate this in her workplace. However, she articulated this risk in relation to the criminal implications of selling such products rather than the possibility of harm to her clients. This was echoed by Brandon, as he recounted his approach to managing risk within the gym setting:

> If I chat with people regularly and establish a level of trust, I'm happy to sell to them. Or if someone I already sell stuff to vouches for them. But if some random geezer comes in the gym and asks, I play naïve and act like I don't know what they're talking about. For all I know, they could be the police … If I don't trust them, they aren't buying anything. It's as simple as that. If I got caught selling [M2 products], I'd lose my job and probably get banged up because it's illegal, isn't it? I'm not fussed about the [fragrances] because they look like the real deal. I don't think I'd get in trouble if I got caught. No one cares about that stuff. I'd probably just have them confiscated, but it's not like I ever have a huge amount of stock at once.

Brandon understood the importance of risk management, through restricting sales to trusted individuals and using his legitimate occupation as 'cover' for his illicit activities. His good business acumen made his endeavours a success. A similar modus operandi of restricting sales to avoid encounters with law enforcement agencies has also been evidenced in virtual markets for illicit drug selling (see Tzanetakis et al, 2016; Demant et al, 2020). Similar to Brandon, Lauren's feelings about risk and harm informed her decision to only sell M2 products to customers she had built up a trusting relationship with:

> If I got caught selling lotions, nobody would care. But with the injections or sprays, I'd get in a lot of trouble, so I have to be careful who I sell to. It's just a way to make some extra money. I don't understand when you hear things about people selling this sort of stuff for a buzz. There is no excitement in it at all. I'm constantly worried that I'll end up talking to the wrong person, like a police officer or something. New people always come to the salon, so I need to be careful. It can be exciting to see the results of people using them, but it's no more exciting than seeing their results from using sunbeds.

Brandon and Lauren's narratives of the importance of trust reflect the significant role played by friendships and personal relations in the 'social supply' (Antonopolous and Hall, 2016) of performance and image enhancing drugs (PIEDs) within the gym environment (van de Ven and Mulrooney, 2017). This supplying of products to close friends or those deemed trustworthy was a core aspect for those involved in the offline supply business in and around Beaufort, including for Carys, who exclusively sold and injected counterfeit Botox and dermal fillers to her close friends and most-trusted clients. Her story will be explored in later sections.

Products and services with higher levels of perceived risk often require high levels of trust and mutual respect between the seller and the buyer (Coomber et al, 2015; Antonopoulos and Hall, 2016; van de Ven and Mulrooney, 2017). Throughout the fieldwork, there were several occasions when people unknown to the offline seller approached them actively looking for products. One notable situation involved a man entering Radiance who claimed he had been using sunbeds for six months at a different salon. He claimed to be unsatisfied with the results and wanted to purchase some products from Lauren:

> From my seat I could quite clearly see him; he had fair skin, was around six-foot tall and dressed in shorts and a vest. He said a friend of a friend told him he could buy 'special' tanning products from Lauren at Radiance. I had never seen her so quiet. Having momentarily been unnerved, she proceeded to tell him she did not have any 'special' products. After a lengthy discussion she sold him a bottle of (counterfeit) tanning lotion and provided him with a 'tanning plan'[1] to be used in her salon. She then told him that if he was unsatisfied with the results at the end of his plan, she would re-discuss his options. This tactic enabled Lauren time to build a trusting relationship. (fieldnote)

Lauren's process and mindset shed light upon how products with higher levels of perceived risk can be more difficult to purchase without a pre-existing relationship. While some sellers can be motivated by a care for, and concern with, helping their clients succeed (Paoli and Donati, 2014; Antonopoulos and Hall, 2016), Lauren's narrative elucidated a lack of concern for the health and wellbeing of others and that the pursuit of profit was her central concern. She admitted to viewing M2 products as 'higher risk' but, like other offline sellers, this was always framed in terms of the possibility of criminal implications rather than through a risk of harming those using these products.

Furthermore, Brandon, discussing other risk management methods, emphasized how his muscular physique played a crucial role in the success of his business, particularly in deterring potential buyers from reporting his illicit business to the gym owner or authorities:

> I think the way I look helps with business. Being big and muscular is the new power and wealth. People are scared to mess with a big lad like me. I'm far from scary, though, I wouldn't hurt a fly. But people don't know that, and in a way, I like that people can be a bit intimidated by

> me. It means they won't try to do one over on me. If I were a skinny little lad, then people would probably be more likely to try and fuck me over … It helps with [PT] work too. You want someone to train you who looks like they know what they're doing. I've got a bit of a reputation at the gym as being successful, being an entrepreneur, and being the type of lad you wouldn't want to get on the wrong side of.

Brandon's statement captures how physical intimidation can be used as a tactic to maintain control and clandestineness. Although he had not been involved in any form of violence, he utilized his body to help establish and maintain a successful business. In an occupation that values the construction and projection of a muscular physique, high levels of respect can be obtained through the aesthetic exterior of the body. The contemporary body has become a focus of investment and improvement for the late-capitalist subject as it can convey several beneficial characteristics for 'competitive circulation' (Wernick, 1991: 193). Brandon's muscular physique is imbued with what Ellis (2016: 88) terms as 'symbolic weaponry'. Such weaponry goes beyond the body's functional capacity to suggest intimidation, violence and power (Kotzé and Antonopoulos, 2019; Cranswick et al, 2020; Gibbs, 2023).

Additionally, Brandon and Lauren both capture how risky patterns of consumption associated with image enhancement drugs are becoming a normalized and widespread pursuit in some legitimate spaces. As Lauren indicates, the use and supply of M2 products in the tanning salon appeared to be culturally accepted and an inherent part of the socio-cultural landscape:

> Since the owner opened a second salon, I've pretty much been running [Radiance]. I've got a great relationship with her, so she trusts me to get on with it. She's always dropping me a text if she's going to pop in, which is handy as it gives me time to hide the stuff in my car. I usually keep them [M2 products] in my car anyway and only get out what I know will be sold within those few hours … Five other people work here. They are all quite young and have no idea. There are usually only two or three of us working in the shop at any given time, so it's fairly easy to sell them without anyone noticing. Especially as we stock normal lotions here … Some of them [customers] take them [injections] home to use, but most end up using them in the sunbed rooms or toilets. If they take their rubbish home, I don't mind.

Brandon possessed a similar operation to Lauren, where injecting practices often took place in 'discreet places' within the gym environment:

Brandon: I sometimes sell them to good mates outside the gym or to gym members who can't come pick them up for whatever reason. I'll drop them off to them if they're local. I don't mind doing that. Most of my sales are made here, though. A lot of people use them in the changing rooms if it's not too busy, or they use them in the toilets or the sunbed room at the back ... There is a group of lads I sell to in the evening. They are all into bodybuilding and train together quite a lot. They are proper good mates, and when they finish their session, they all go up to the changing rooms after their workout and inject [M2 products] together before they head home.

Sam: Do the other staff know?

Brandon: No way. It's all kept very hush. I would get fired if the boss found out. I don't sell to many people, but those lads I do sell to are my most regular customers. They come and train around an hour and a half before closing, and I'm often the one who closes the gym, so I can monitor it. Sometimes it's [another staff member] closing, but she can't go into the male changing room, so she doesn't have a clue. I just go up and check before they leave, just in case they've left something behind. But they never do. If they did and someone else caught them, they knew they would get banned from the gym. And have you seen them? Big lads. The gym is their life so they wouldn't take that risk. They are all proper sound.

Brandon's words demonstrate how legitimate occupations constitute a platform on which opportunities for illegal business and risky patterns of consumption can present themselves. This reality echoes some examples within the existing literature (Antonopoulos and Hall, 2016; Gibbs, 2023), whereby there was an easy distribution of lifestyle drugs in some gyms, and drug-injecting practices had become 'normalized and an inherent part of the socio-cultural landscape' (Antonopoulos and Hall, 2016: 12). Therefore, risky patterns of consumption associated with these products are becoming increasingly normalized in legitimate spaces (Coomber et al, 2015; Hall, 2019).

Motivations for selling

Selling and administering illicit beauty in the home

Alongside the normalization of consuming these products in legitimate spaces outside of the home, there is also an increasing consumption of such products within the home. During my time in the field, I met Carys. In a similar fashion to Lauren and Brandon, Carys used her legitimate beauty profession as a 'front' to sell illicit products to existing clients and close friends. While working as a mobile hairdresser in and around Beaufort, she identified the opportunity to make some extra money within the boundaries of her occupation, administering Botox and dermal fillers. Carys began buying (counterfeit) facial injectables to improve her appearance. However, after a year of self-injecting she decided to offer the illicit service to existing hairdressing clients and her close friends within the context of a 'Botox party'.[2] Having known the host (Reanne, 28) of the Botox parties since school, I was fortunate enough to obtain an invitation to one. Before the party, I was invited into a WhatsApp group called the 'Clique',[3] which posted the message: 'Botox Party @ 6pm. Bring Prosecco'. The following fieldnote sheds light on the first Botox party I attended:

> It was a Friday evening at the end of September, and I was attending my first Botox party. As I arrived at Reanne's apartment, located just outside of Beaufort, the atmosphere was filled with lively chatter. Reanne turned the music down slightly and introduced me to the others. They all looked relatively young and very fashionable. Jessica (22) was dressed in a Gucci T-shirt and black jeans with knee-high black boots. Olivia had a wide-legged jumpsuit on and was a lot taller than the others. Elle was wearing a tartan dress, and Grace (18) had a short denim skirt on with a strappy black vest. They all had a designer bag carefully placed either on their lap or in front of them: Louis Vuitton, Marc Jacobs or Mulberry. Earlier in the day, Carys had messaged the group chat to say she would be late as she had a hair client. We all piled around the large dining room table while we waited, and a magnum of Prosecco was passed around. I poured a glass and passed it on. It was the first time I had met the other women, and they were surprisingly very welcoming. We all sat around the table for about an hour, drinking and talking.
>
> Carys walked through the door around 7.15 pm and shouted: 'Who's ready to look good ladies? I bet you're all buzzing!' She looked just as fashionable as the others. Dressed in a tight black midi dress, Carys was slim with long blonde hair tied back into a ponytail. After a few minutes of small talk, Carys went into the adjoining living room to set up. She placed the products on the small side table by the sofa. It looked like the real party was about to begin. During the evening I had limited opportunities to chat with Carys about her injecting practices. Although I knew she was a hairdresser, I did not know whether she had previously worked in a medical profession; at this point, I did not know much about her. Despite her assertion that you do not have to be a medical professional to provide and administer the products, the fact no one at the party signed a consent form before they received an injection indicated that she was not a qualified or licensed medic but was more than willing to provide

> Botox and dermal fillers to others without an official consultation with a prescriber. As Carys did not seem in the mood to talk on this occasion, I did not want to probe her too much and jeopardize an invitation to the next Botox party. I kept in contact with the group and remained part of their WhatsApp group. They invited me to several of their gatherings, including further Botox parties, pamper nights and nights out on the town. As I started to attend more events, Carys became more talkative and was more forthcoming about her illicit actions and the motivations behind them. (fieldnote)

Carys had worked in the beauty industry for eight years and had been self-employed as a mobile hairdresser for four of those. She left school at 16 and worked in a supermarket for a few years, before completing a course to become a qualified hairdresser. Carys had then worked in a hair salon for four years but wanted a job with more freedom and flexibility. As mobile hairdressing appeared to tick most boxes, she started her own business where she was able to achieve a high degree of autonomy with her working days. Having an existing business in the beauty industry offered Carys the correct entrepreneurial skills to pursue profit and merge her legal and illegal practices. It provided her with the platform and opportunity to offer an additional service to her existing clients under the guise of mobile hairdressing. Carys explained:

> Hairdressing can be quite unpredictable in terms of how busy I get. I go through periods without any stable income, and if I didn't have this business on the side, I wouldn't be able to do the things I want in life. Half of my hairdressing clients also get an injection done at the same appointment. It's handy because sometimes clients want filler or Botox, and they're like 'I may as well get my hair cut too', so it's extra money for me. And it's handy to have the hairdressing as a cover just in case someone did get suspicious. I can just tell them I'm a mobile hairdresser.

Driven partially by the precarity of income and stable work from her mobile hairdressing business, Carys viewed this as a convenient way to supplement income and improve her financial situation. Such precarious employment conditions have made selling beauty products through personal networks appeal to many women (Carr and Kelan, 2023). In fact, the UK government has recently urged job seekers to consider roles in the beauty industry (Department for Work and Pensions, 2023). Nevertheless, compared to Brandon and Lauren, Carys seemed less interested in making a profit. Her primary motivations appeared to be helping others enhance their appearance and maintaining friendships:

> I wanted to get Botox, but it was too expensive. A friend told me she knew someone who sold the products fairly cheap, and she put me in contact with her. She taught me how to inject them myself, but I also spent a lot of time watching various YouTube videos. Some of my friends wanted to get it done, but like me, they couldn't afford it. And it just spiralled from there. I started injecting a few close friends, like Reanne, and it just transformed into a Botox party. Reanne invited her friend, who then invited a few of their friends. We then grew into a very close friendship group. At the first few parties, I didn't let anyone drink. It wasn't worth the risk, and back then, I was so nervous injecting others. You don't want to fuck it up … I've been doing it for a few years now, and I'm a lot more relaxed. I let them drink what they want. I wait until I've finished doing all their injections before I have a drink though, and then enjoy a glass of something while I do my own.

In my first conversation with Carys, she assured me that non-medical professionals can provide and administer the products. It later transpired that Carys was unaware of the illicit nature of her activities:

> I've always bought them from the same person. I don't know where she gets them from, but it can be hard to get hold of unless you're a medical professional or something. She lives about forty minutes away, so I can easily buy products as and when I need them. When I first bought them from her, I thought she was qualified to give them to me. I thought it was all legit. I know the products aren't the real deal, but it doesn't bother me or the girls. There has never been an issue and I'd been using them for a year before I knew. It does the same job, what's the difference.

Although Carys was initially adamant that she was not aware, she then acknowledged that she was 'not too concerned' about using and injecting herself and others with the counterfeit products as she 'had never had a problem'. As such, the supply and consumption of these products appeared to rest on the fact she had not seen any adverse reactions or problems. While it is difficult to tell if Carys was telling the truth, it is also possible that she may not have known that the provider of the products was not a registered medical professional.

When Botox and dermal fillers are injected by someone without any medical training,[4] in an atmosphere where alcohol consumption is present, and the products are counterfeit, the medical uncertainties surrounding facial injectable use are heightened (Cook and Dwyer, 2017). The first time Carys began injecting others, she would not allow them to consume alcohol. However, as she became more confident administering the products, the dangers became obscured and these women evolved into a close-knit group of friends, changing the supplier–consumer relationship. Although Carys would not consume alcohol until after she had injected others, those being injected would usually have 2–3 glasses of Prosecco before their procedures. Consequently, these Botox parties were fraught with a whole host of new dangers, risks and potential harms related to the (counterfeit) product itself (for example, swelling, haemorrhaging or paralysing of the respiratory muscles) and the administrative context (Cook and Dwyer, 2017). Carys understood that using facial injectables could be more serious and damaging when combined with alcohol consumption. However, she also justified her injecting practices by claiming that counterfeits are just as harmful as non-counterfeits. Compared to medical fields that provide strict guidelines and standards set by regulatory bodies, the regulation for Botox and dermal fillers is less robust with no requirements for registration.

Alongside the perceived safety of being injected by a trusted individual, and building on the theoretical concepts discussed in Chapter 2, the informal nature and setting of the parties were certainly factors in why it was easy for the potential for harm to be fetishistically disavowed by these young women. Additionally, cosmetic enhancement products are becoming 'run-of-the-mill', they are now relatively affordable, easily accessible in familiar environments and perceived as being as important as regular body upkeep such as teeth cleaning, haircuts and having a manicure (Berkowitz, 2017; Cook and Dwyer, 2017). As the use and supply of these products are moving into everyday environments, such products and procedures have become decontextualized and dislocated from medical contexts. This has led some cosmetic enhancements to evolve into everyday products, normalizing them further and masking their potential for dangers (Cook and Dwyer, 2017).

David: from drug dealing to counterfeit selling

David was diametrically different from other sellers within this fieldwork. He was the only seller who was not a consumer of beauty and enhancement products; he was not embedded within the beauty and self-improvement culture, and his life history and motivations for selling differed from the others as he had a family to financially support. The following fieldnote recalls his route into selling counterfeit fragrances:

> Arriving at the pub in East London, which was David's local, I saw he was standing at the bar with a pint in hand. David possessed a friendly demeanour. He was around six feet tall, his build was fairly slim, and he wore jeans, a plain blue T-shirt and trainers that looked like they had seen better days. Unlike the other sellers, David was not interested in the latest fashion trends or designer items, and he would only buy

> clothing items he desperately needed, rather than simply desired. I only met David a few times due to other commitments in his life, but when we did, I sat and listened to him for about three hours. He was aware of my research and was keen to talk about how his life experiences had led him to his current situation. After around ten minutes of talking, David began to run me through his career trajectory. He worked a part-time job in the hospitality sector, which was his main source of employment and sold counterfeit fragrances on the streets of London. Before this, David worked in a series of jobs with few prospects, low wages and limited hours through zero-hour contracts. He opened up about how he had endured instances of relative deprivation, humiliation and emotional suffering throughout his life. This led him to become involved in various illegal markets. (fieldnote)

Reflecting on his time growing up, David regularly truanted from school and became acquainted with a network of individuals involved in the cannabis trade:

> I grew up on the estate with my mum. We were that family who never really had much. It's not like she didn't try and provide for us. It just never worked out. We didn't have the easiest of lives. I lost my dad at a young age, and we went from being financially stable to having fuck all. It was so shit for her, and I just wanted to take the pressure off. I hated school, started skipping classes, and eventually began selling weed on the estate. After a while, I was able to branch out a bit more around the town and got some new turf to sell on. I hated doing it. But it did help us, and we could live a bit more comfortably.

After leaving school at the age of sixteen with a lack of qualifications, David drifted between a range of jobs at call centres and in the hospitality sector, though he did not work at them for very long due to his 'shit work ethic'. From the handful of times I met David, he was always very quick to justify his actions and reasons for becoming embroiled in drug dealing. He had been a committed drug dealer for many years, but in recent years has distanced himself from selling drugs:

David: I left education too young and didn't have my head screwed on properly, you know the future just seemed so far away. All I wanted was to take some pressure off my mum and get us off the estate. It wasn't a nice place. When I was selling weed, I ended up losing my job in the call centre because I had such a shit work ethic. It was my fault, but even to this day, call centres don't want to hire me. Past David was a right twat.

Sam: What made you stop dealing?

David: My girlfriend at the time got pregnant and I knew I needed to get out of the game. As soon as it became a class B drug, and the police got more on the ball with busting people, I called it a day. I had just had a kid and it was no longer worth the risk. It all changes when you've got other people to think about. That's when I started to sell [fragrances].

Sam: Have you been selling them for long?

David: I've been selling them for a few years. It's not ideal but it does help. One of the lads I used to deal with started selling loads of fake designer gear. Clothes, perfumes and aftershaves. I tried so hard to find a full-time job but had no luck. It's a tough world out there; no one gives people like me a chance. I started helping him sell some of his stock because I needed the extra income and didn't want to go back to selling gear. I then got my job as a kitchen porter, but it was only part-time. So, I sell the [fragrances] too, but I don't work for my mate anymore. He still gets the products for me, but I buy them from him at the standard price and then sell them for more. I haven't stopped looking for a better job though. As soon as I get a proper full-time job, I'll go fully legit.

The dual effects of the reclassification of cannabis and the responsibilities of parenthood forced David to stop selling cannabis due to the risks. After several failed attempts at finding secure, full-time employment, the opportunity arose for David to sell counterfeit fragrances. David was very charismatic, and although he had no specific or personal connections to a beauty-related environment like the other sellers, he would visit various pubs and markets looking for people interested in buying the products. There was no real structure to his selling, and in contrast to the other sellers in this study, David had no contact with his customers outside of his illegal transaction.

One notable aspect that emerged from discussions with David was the importance placed upon his temporary position in the illicit world. It was not part of his life, his identity or a means to earn money for excessive consumption. Rather, it was perfunctory. David's motivations for peddling such products were for subsistence. He detested his position as a small-time criminal and, in stark contrast to the sellers within this research and within other studies (Hobbs, 1995; Hall et al, 2008), he did not consider himself to be a profit-motivated entrepreneur; selling illicit products and being in that world was not integral to his identity and status. His limited experience in the legitimate labour market did not seem to restrain his aspirations of owning a catering company by the time he reached age thirty.

Doing illicit business from a young age

Lauren, the manager of Radiance, showed early indications of possessing the type of business acumen that was later to make her, as she described herself, a 'successful businesswoman'. At the age of 13 Lauren sold confectionary items during break times at her school:

> I used to get 80p for a packet of crisps and between 50p and £1 for chocolate. They didn't sell any junk food in my school, so I saw an opportunity to make money. I'd use my pocket money to buy it from the local newsagent. I probably earned about £5 profit per day.

Lauren left school as soon as the law allowed and obtained a full-time job at a hair salon sweeping floors, answering the phone and making tea. This income was insufficient, so she obtained a second job collecting glasses at a local pub on Friday and Saturday nights. Much of her income, then as now, was spent on fashion and beauty goods. Shortly after, Lauren was offered a Saturday job at Radiance by her friend's sister, who is the owner of the tanning salon. She continued to work all three jobs until she was offered a full-time position at Radiance. Around a year later, the owner of Radiance opened a second shop just outside of the county and Lauren became the manager of Radiance. As Lauren started to sell illicit goods, her desire to become a businesswoman and earn more money grew. Yet she had no time to take on additional legitimate work, so she sought opportunities to earn money within the setting of her legitimate occupation (Hobbs, 1995; Antonopoulos and Hall, 2016).

Brandon, the self-employed PT, also exercised good business acumen from a young age. Brandon's childhood endeavours have helped him formulate his entrepreneurial career. He described his time growing up as 'far from the ordinary' as he spent many of his childhood years in and out of local authority care, before finding a permanent foster family. Brandon's foster family owned a fruit and vegetable stall at a market, which he worked on at the weekend:

> I'd stand there all day Saturday shouting my head off. I was about 13 when they first let me on the stall. They thought I was doing it for fun, but I did such a good job they gave me some money for it. And then it became a proper job. On my break, I'd wander around the market and always chat to a man who had a stall with his wife. He was sound. Spending every weekend at the market, you get to know the other traders well. The stall sold a range of health and beauty stuff and he told me about the profit he earned on the designer [fragrances]. The sprays he sold were all fake. I think I was like 14 at this point and I was

> a cocky fucker. We had a joke that if I could sell a box of aftershaves he was getting rid of, I could keep the profit. So, I took them, sold them to my mates and that's how it started. I went back to him the next week and bought some with the money I had earned. Sold them and it went from there.

Brandon had always been fixated on accumulating enough money to purchase the material and symbolic possessions denied to him as a child. He experienced and learnt knowledge in legal and illegal practices that earned him a reasonable income, providing him with the freedom and money he had always desired. The experiences and accounts of both Brandon and Lauren are by no means unique. Hobbs's (1988) study on illicit entrepreneurship in the East End of London also found that those demonstrating good business acumen at an early age would often be aided by these experiences, leading to greater levels of success in their illicit endeavours later in life.

The symbolic value of being an entrepreneur

Traditionally, consumers and suppliers were seen as distinct roles in economic transactions. However, the emergence of a trend in 'prosumption' (Beer and Burrows, 2010; Ritzer and Jurgenson, 2010) means that individuals or entities, such as small business owners or freelancers, can find themselves both supplying goods or services and being consumers of other goods or services, creating a more fluid and interconnected dynamic. As such, the blurred boundaries between the producer and the consumer allow individuals, such as Craig, to move flexibly between the two positions in the pursuit of their consumer lifestyle.

When I met Craig, he had been selling counterfeits for two years and had over 20,000 Instagram followers. He started selling small quantities of fashion counterfeits to his close friends, which involved him purchasing designer T-shirts, bags and accessories online and abroad to sell in the offline world. After one year, Craig moved his illicit endeavours online to reach a broader audience and expanded the types of products he sold to also include a range of beauty products. He began using eBay but soon realized he could make a larger profit through social media websites. Although quite unresponsive and standoffish when I first made contact, once he realized that we were from the same town and shared some mutual friends he felt more comfortable and agreed to meet in his local pub to discuss his illicit activities.

Craig had a very strong work ethic in terms of his online counterfeit business and often referred to himself as an entrepreneur. He had recently graduated from university with a degree in history and worked full-time in a bar just outside of Beaufort. The plan, in his mind, was simple: 'to earn a lot of money, quit the full-time job and become self-employed'.

Craig lived with three friends in rented accommodation and the cost of his rent was considerable, especially considering his employment at the bar earned him less than £15,000 per year. With the cost of rent continuously increasing, Craig's wages barely covered his outgoing costs, prompting him to supplement his income through selling counterfeits:

> I just started buying bits here and there for me and my mates and then more people seemed interested in it, and I saw an opportunity to sell them and make some cash. I needed extra money. All my income was going on rent … I'm not doing anyone any harm. I honestly don't see it as a crime. I'm just helping people buy stuff they wouldn't otherwise be able to afford.

During the two years of fieldwork, it was not unusual for Craig to talk about his aspirations of becoming a successful entrepreneur. He admitted that as his business in the illicit sphere developed, he became more inclined to refer to himself as an entrepreneur, which, in his opinion, carried high status and rewards:

> It's about being successful and having the guts to take a risk. As soon as you hear someone describe themselves as an entrepreneur or a businessman, you automatically think intelligent, clever and cool. Even if you're an employee for a cool company like Supreme, it just isn't as cool as being like 'I'm an entrepreneur'. It just screams success and independence. If I met someone and they asked what I do, I wouldn't tell them I'm a barman. It isn't who I am or what I'm about. I'm not going to be doing it long-term … I'm a businessman, an entrepreneur.

Craig was clear that although he had a 'real' job in the legitimate sector, his occupation was never something that defined him. He developed an entrepreneurial status that was in no way bound to his occupation in the service sector, highlighting how being an 'entrepreneur' is validated by its recognition and formalization on social media and not by his skills or intrinsic progression (Smith, 2014; Raymen, 2018). Having a distinct identity was important to Craig, and he often spoke about the pleasures associated with being an active entrepreneurial risk-taker. In his mind, being an entrepreneur was a vocation central to his everyday life, associated with freedom, independence, self-achievement and status. This theme was common across all the participants, where some constructed themselves as 'social media influencers' (for example, Olivia) or 'beauty experts' (for example, Carys) on Facebook and Instagram, regardless of not having the correct training or a large social media following. This finding echoes Raymen's (2018) ethnographic work on parkour, where most of his participants described themselves as a 'professional freerunner' on their social media accounts despite having 'real' jobs in the service economy.

Although Craig worked full-time in a bar, he did not view himself in the same way as he viewed his colleagues. He would often elevate his entrepreneurial activities to occupy a higher position from which he could perceive himself as looking down on the 'losers' stranded in the low-status sector. For Craig, bar work was not a long-term option, it was a brief stop on his path to personal success, prosperity and greater things:

> Everyone who works at the bar hates it. It's shit hours, shit pay and you have to deal with drunk idiots all the time. I couldn't get through each day at the bar knowing that's it for me, that's my life and I'm stuck there. At least I can say I'm an entrepreneur with big plans and I'm going to make something of myself … I'm not a loser who works in a bar full-time. And the way it's all going, I'll be out of the bar soon. And then I can finally focus more on my business and becoming successful.

Although Craig often talked as if he occupied a higher position, there was a premature quality to this. Craig was not in the financial position to leave his full-time job anytime soon. Despite this, Craig continued to make plans based on these assumptions and perceived himself to be on the road to success. Work at the bar was only useful as it provided Craig with funds for his illicit business and helped pay off some of his existing debt; the job itself had no bearing on his identity.

Brandon, too, was quick to introduce himself as an entrepreneur. Brandon had sold counterfeit perfumes during his teens but over the last two years he had started selling M2 products as the money earned from selling perfumes promptly became inadequate for the enhanced lifestyle he desired:

> Before I was 18 I hadn't even been out of the country. I didn't get holidays and nice things that other people grew up with. That's why I started selling [fragrances] to my mates. I saved the money I made so that one day I could have a better life. When I turned 18, I went on the classic lads' holiday, got some half-decent clothes and moved in with my girlfriend's family until we had enough money to rent our own place. I wanted more and that's when I looked into selling tanning injections. I knew I could make a lot of money with that, and the risks were completely overshadowed by the money … Combined with my PT business, it brings in a decent income.

The monetary gains from selling illicit goods offered Brandon a taste of the lifestyle he had always desired, replete with fashionable clothes, nights out, holidays and material possessions that were out of reach throughout his childhood. The more money Brandon earned, the more he was fixated on accumulating enough money to buy consumer items. His involvement in selling illicit goods appeared to be a direct result of his time growing up and his desire to be immersed in a world of excessive consumerism. However, his inexhaustible desire to indulge in continuous consumption appeared to be tangled in a web of narcissism and egoism. Being able to go on holiday, go to expensive bars and buy the latest gadgets was a way to manifest his accomplishments and prove to himself that he had become a successful entrepreneur. Other sellers (Lauren, Craig and Carys) also bought into the interconnected ethos of entrepreneurialism and consumption.

As deviant leisure scholars have suggested, more people now engage in hedonistic leisure pursuits as an important appendage to their sense of self-esteem and existential security, rather than to simply rest and reinvigorate (Smith, 2014; Hayward and Turner, 2019). The following observation elucidates how individuals relish the opportunity to not only spend their wages but also to display their accomplishments and elevate the self by inspiring envy in others (Hall et al, 2008):

> Following an early morning gym session, Brandon invited me over to see some of the products he sold. His flat, where he and his partner lived, was only a short walk from the gym. As I entered his home, Brandon was very keen to point out their latest purchases, how much they spent on items and that they were all branded, authentic items. Brandon had never been shy about the fact he spends a large amount of his income on material and symbolic possessions or the fact he was deeply concerned with his presentation. As I sat in his living room sipping on a coffee, I was faced with a range of expensive items: a cinematic 65-inch TV mounted on the wall, various gaming consoles and an Apple computer squeezed into the corner. Brandon proceeded to show me around the rest of his flat. It was clear the tour was not informative but rather a very calculated tactic by providing a display of commodities that evidenced his life as a success, and that he was succeeding as a prosperous entrepreneur. His desire to spend his earnings on 'must-have' commodities was a way to manifest his accomplishments. Attaining an entrepreneurial status and a meaningful sense of identity appeared to be his raison d'être. (fieldnote)

Although Brandon spent his profits on material and symbolic goods that enhanced his entrepreneurial status to help him secure more work (as a PT and selling illicit goods), he also regularly expressed a genuine interest in the aesthetic progression of others, which was not surprising considering his occupation in the fitness industry. He was one of the popular PTs at the gym and appeared to train the most clients. Brandon was well respected in the fitness scene and many attendees admired his physique and entrepreneurial flair. He had a range of promotional merchandise (for example, gym vests, business cards, hoodies) produced for his PT business and spent a great deal of time on his licit and illicit businesses. Brandon's effort and aesthetic qualities were a credible source of capital that could be used to secure business, gain symbolic capital and secure a high degree of social standing within the gym and more broadly within the enterprise culture. He had reached an elevated entrepreneurial status which many young people envied and admired.

Chapter summary

Sellers involved in the counterfeit business in the UK are often self-employed entrepreneurs (see Antonopoulos et al, 2018) rather than individuals manipulated by so-called 'organized crime groups' as official accounts continue to suggest (Europol, 2013). The varied motivations and drivers for selling, along with the sellers' positions as consumers, are centred on their identity, appearance and desire to consume, and, as such, do not fit within the traditional explanatory frameworks for selling counterfeits that often dominate criminology's theoretical repertoire. This is particularly the case for research that places the marginalized impoverished subject at its centre, or the 'organized criminal' who is going to invest the proceeds purely into illegal activities. For David, it was more about subsistence, and he was clear about detesting his position as a small-time criminal. An accompanying perception is that a clear boundary exists between legal and illegal markets, separating the 'upperworld' and the underworld (van Duyne, 2005).

The motivations of the participants contrasted sharply with the common assumptions associated with the supply of illicit drugs and counterfeits. For most of the participants (Lauren, Craig, Brandon and Carys) the selling of illicit beauty products and services provided an income that funded their consumer lifestyles. Furthermore, the feel-good factor of 'helping' others (for example, Brandon) and maintaining friendships (for example, Carys) also underpinned their practices. Their continued efforts within the legitimate economy suggest they were not nihilistic criminals bound to some form of criminal underworld (Salinas, 2018). They worked hard in both legitimate and illegitimate spheres because they wanted to better their situations, increase their income and, ultimately, be perceived as entrepreneurially inclined by their peers. In this sense, the selling of illicit beauty products and services were entirely congruent with, and conformist to, the values of neoliberalism. Finally, it became clear how the interconnection between the online and offline supply of counterfeit products was reshaping the beauty industry and how online marketplaces played a crucial role in the illicit beauty trade at the local level.

5

Consuming (Counterfeit) Beauty; Consuming Aesthetic Pleasure

Introduction

This chapter will focus on the consumption of counterfeit and illicit beauty products, including how consumers buy counterfeits, the importance and symbolic value of buying branded beauty and the contexts in which cosmetic enhancements are used. Alongside this, the broader instrumental motivations that drive the research participants' beauty consumption will be examined, including how beauty and bodily enhancement products are an act of self-transformation connected to professional and socio-economic success. In this chapter I assess the lived experiences of consumer lifestyles in the context of an absence of meaningful opportunities for fulfilling employment in order to examine the extent to which young people are governed by competition and hyper-comparison. This work provides an extensive view of the nature of beauty and counterfeit consumption to exemplify some of the harms generated from commitment to and conformity with the norms and values of consumer culture in late-capitalist society.

Far from adulting

As set out in Chapter 2, the significant restructuring of both the economic and political sphere in the UK has impacted young people's entry and initial experiences of paid labour. Compared to previous generations in which there was a relative fixity in relation to geography and jobs across a working life (Kumar, 1988), many young people are forced to take insecure and low-paid work, often within the service sector, and generally experience greater levels of precarity across their working lives (Kalleberg and Vallas, 2018). The idea of spending an entire working life in the same job was not only unappealing for most of the participants, it was also unlikely, as stable and secure employment among these groups is a relic of the past (Lloyd, 2013). The labour market has been characterized by flexibility and insecurity, and individuals are expected to change jobs up to ten times per career (Fenton and Demott, 2006). Throughout the fieldwork, all but one of the participants were in legitimate employment, and, for most, remaining employed proved to be a precarious task. However, even for the person out of work (Liam), securing a job was equally as trying (see Southwood, 2011).

Across all of the research participants there was a noticeable consistency in their prioritization of their consumer and leisure experiences over their work. This was perhaps expected, considering most of the participants worked in jobs with few prospects, poor pay and limited hours through zero-hour contracts. The examples that follow are illustrative of many of the participants' experiences. Jessica worked full-time in a café that was persistently looking to reduce her hours. Both Sophie and Carys were self-employed in the beauty industry and described their jobs as precarious, so they both endeavoured to earn money through other avenues: Carys offered a (counterfeit) Botox and dermal filler service alongside her hairdressing business, and Sophie was attempting to be a full-time social media influencer through her Instagram fitness page while working as a self-employed eyelash artist. Liam (25) worked full-time in London for the first 3 months of the fieldwork before being made redundant due to staff cuts. Reanne worked a series of part-time, temporary jobs in retail before finding something she described as 'long-term':

> I've gone from job to job. I always end up with temp jobs on zero-hour contracts, so I have to constantly keep searching for jobs. It's been hard to get anything permanent and secure. I'm on a long-term contract now though. It's between nine months and a year covering maternity leave, which gives me a rest from applying for other jobs.

Reanne was a retail worker who had been stuck on temporary contracts. She bought various counterfeit and non-counterfeit make-up products and clothing items from social media sellers, had undergone various cosmetic surgeries and regularly hosted the (counterfeit) Botox parties for the 'Clique', a female friendship group of beauty consumers. Since leaving school, Reanne had been in and out of work, and the limited labour market opportunities meant she viewed her temporary contract in a positive light. This mindset was common across the wider participants and echoes a similar finding from Raymen (2018), where a three-month contract was considered 'long-term'. The precariousness in young people's employments and lack of financial stability can distort and destabilize their idea of the future in late modernity. As such, in lieu of making the future plans necessary for completing their transition to adulthood, young people are postponing such a transition and instead are drawn to leisure and consumer circuits for their identity formation and status affirmation (Lloyd, 2012).

Reanne rented a two-bedroom apartment just outside of Beaufort. She lived alone and had a whole room dedicated to 'getting ready', with a range of expensive items that cemented her commitment to consumerism: there was a Dyson hairdryer, a large collection of designer clothes, shoes and accessories, and display shelves full of high-end beauty products. Her commitment to consumerism and sustained attachment to upholding a presence within her friendship group diverted her from progressing towards adulthood:

> I'm spending so much money at the moment, and I should really be saving for a house … I suppose it's more that I feel like I should grow up. Minus my job, I do like the lifestyle I live. And if I started trying to be an adult, then I wouldn't be able to spend as much money as I do on myself or be the person I am now. I'm in my twenties I want to go out, spend money on myself, and just make myself feel good. Without any of that, I wouldn't really have anything real in life. It's not like I have a booming career or anything. Sure, it's a narcissistic way of living, but it's nice to have the freedom to be the best version of myself.

Reanne's desire to conspicuously display her lifestyle and identity as part of her friendship group was, by her own admission, underpinned by narcissism. As the absence of stability impedes future plans, it becomes more appealing for young people to immerse themselves within the immediacy of consumer markets as a means of maintaining a semblance of cultural success. The lack of choice around job opportunities made it increasingly difficult for the participants to plan for the future, leaving them little choice but to stay in the 'extended present' (Nowotny, 1994). Aware of the harsh reality of the future and the difficulty in finding secure employment and settling down, planning for the future was undesirable. As such, ambitions were limited to maintaining employment, friendships and immersing themselves in consumer markets and indebtedness as they continued to live 'deferred lives' (Davis and Cartwright, 2019). This is reflected in Lloyd's (2012: 630) ethnographic work among call-centre workers, where participants chose to 'dim their horizons and live for the present' instead of facing the difficulties of the future.

Despite the participants being aged between 18 and 29 years old, they all described their situations as 'far from adulting'. This theme was particularly visible in Reanne's narrative:

> I didn't think that at the age of 26, I'd be living alone in rented accommodation with absolutely no job security, career or boyfriend. I always thought I'd be successful in something, maybe even engaged, with a house. But I'm far from adulting. I just got stuck working in

> the retail sector, and you can't exactly meet a lad in a women's clothing store. As much as I dislike my job, it does pay the bills. It's just not something I want to do forever. Part of me is like, OK Reanne, it's time to grow up and sort your shit out. But at the same time, I don't feel ready to grow up. I haven't exactly got a plan for the future. And even when I try to make a plan, it doesn't work out because I'm jumping from temp job to temp job. It's so hard to get anything secure, and to be honest, I've stopped trying so hard. I think that's why I love having the girls over each weekend. It gives me a purpose and makes me feel important. I'm the glue that holds the group together, and they wouldn't be friends if I didn't have the gatherings. But I'm not exactly going to be hosting them when I'm like 40 … For now, I'm just focusing on myself and my appearance. At least I can control that.

Even those who had attempted the transition from youth to adulthood through moving out of their family home, getting a job or becoming financially independent branded their transition to adulthood as an unsteady and transient experience. Olivia (25), for example, was financially independent and purchased a range of counterfeit and non-counterfeit make-up products and clothing items from social media sellers. She had undergone various cosmetic surgeries and regularly attended the (counterfeit) Botox parties as part of the Clique. Olivia moved out of her family home when she worked as a model. Following a career change, Olivia had to move back home as she attempted to make her big break in the world of social media as an influencer. This provided her with a less stable and steady source of income, making her far from comfortable financially. Similarly, shortly after Liam graduated from university, he obtained his 'dream' job in London and relocated from his hometown in the Midlands to a commuter town just outside of London. Following redundancy, Liam was reluctant to move back to his family home as he had become drawn to the social and cultural possibilities of the city. His story will be explored in more detail later in the chapter, but by the end of the fieldwork Liam had to move back to his family home and worked a job in the retail sector; he continued the lifestyle he had previously lived with his school friends who similarly found themselves moving back to their hometown after graduating.

Throughout the fieldwork, I encountered multiple examples in which the participants felt their experiences oscillated between adulthood and adolescence as their attempts to make a complete transition ended with them drifting between and across the boundaries of adulthood. Such experiences are emblematic of what Fisher (2009) terms as 'reflexive impotence'. This was evident throughout Craig's account, as he attempted to navigate the increasingly challenging transition into adulthood but became distracted by and drawn to more valuable avenues of identification. Part of Craig's idea of himself as an entrepreneur, rather than a barman, was reflected in his desire to spend money in the pursuit of status, distinction and social prestige, irrespective of how these bouts of spending would impinge upon his financial security (Smith, 2014).

For Craig, spending money was about attaining an identity as an entrepreneur. He would purposefully erase any possibility of personal failure from the agenda and continued to convince himself that he was an entrepreneur. Rather than face the difficult reality of his financial situation or the fact he was trapped at the bottom of the labour market, it became easier for Craig to fantasize about the 'big break' that would transform his life and provide him with the entrepreneurial status he believed he was destined for. In this sense, Craig's future was on hold, and he had no option but to enjoy the 'extended present' which allowed him the comfort of not facing the reality of a difficult future (Brannen and Nilsen, 2002). Therefore, he had become trapped in an endless quest for money, driven by both an insatiable desire for personal gain and the fear of not maintaining a status associated with success. Hyper-consumption of consumer items and leisure experiences were embraced by most of the participants in hope of stemming the anxiety-inducing insecurity of precarious employment and transition into adulthood.

Taking back control through appearance

As a result of the precariousness of existing labour markets and the dominant presence of a leisure-based economy, the research participants perpetually felt that they had little control over anything other than their appearance. Given how individuals are constantly trying to be better than one another, or at least appear better, in order to be recognized in the physical and virtual world (Honneth, 1996), consumers viewed their appearance as a way to improve job prospects and social standing. As a result, they became drawn to beauty, fitness and bodily enhancement to re-sculpt the body, restructure the self and, ultimately, boost their physical capital in an attempt to retain an element of control of their lives and construct a meaningful sense of identity (Kotzé and Antonopoulos, 2019).

This was reflected in Olivia's account, as engagement with beauty markets became a way for her to try and regain a sense of control over her everyday life. After spending most of her working life as a fitness model, Olivia made the decision to leave the industry to become a full-time 'social media influencer'. By her own admission, she had been fascinated with cosmetic surgery since her early teens. During her childhood, Olivia lacked confidence and described her time at school as a long period of self-loathing as she struggled with her self-image. She had always dreamt of becoming a model and, as her insecurities grew, it began to dawn on her that cosmetic surgery was the only way she could alter her physical attributes, which she often referred to as 'genetic flaws'.

Shortly after her eighteenth birthday, Olivia had a breast augmentation:

> I used to be so insecure about my body shape. I was so skinny, which came with the problem of having a flat chest. I knew getting surgery was the only way I could achieve the body I wanted. It's not like losing weight, where you can diet and exercise. It's a genetic flaw, and my only option was surgery. At that point, modelling was my life. It was the only thing I wanted to do. And before my operation, I would rarely be selected during castings. They didn't want flat-chested girls like me … But even after I had the operation, I still struggled to get work.

After being rejected from many modelling jobs, Olivia was advised that if she wanted to improve her chances in the industry, it would be necessary for her to undergo further cosmetic surgeries and procedures; recommendations included a rhinoplasty, Botox and dermal fillers. Olivia reflected:

> A few years ago, while I was on a job, a few comments were made about my face. They said I had the 'potential' to have a good face for modelling and asked if I had ever considered Botox. It was brutal. And it wasn't the first time I'd been spoken to like that. I'd already considered it, but I didn't think I was in a rush to get it.

Determined to progress in her career, Olivia attuned to the demands of modelling. She spent all her savings from her part-time job, alongside some money she borrowed from her parents, on improving her appearance.

By the age of 21, she had undergone a rhinoplasty, and shortly after she started using Botox and dermal fillers. The spiralling costs and never-ending demands of the modelling industry that stems from the need to alter the body to increase marketability (Entwistle and Wissinger, 2006) were evident from Olivia's words:

> I spent around two hours a day in the gym doing a morning cardio session and a weight-focused session in the afternoon. I ate a very controlled diet too. I'm lucky, though, as I don't put on fat very easily. There is so much that goes into modelling. If I weren't at a casting or the gym, I'd be at some form of beauty appointment. Tanning, waxing, regular trips to the hairdressers … There was a lot of pressure to keep up with appearances. The demands were just never-ending.

Even when Olivia left the modelling industry to focus on a career as a social media influencer, she continued enduring commitments to transforming the body and body maintenance. The surgically enhanced body is connected to socio-economic success on various levels, affecting every aspect of not only what we do but what we think about our lives. This form of pressure and desire for social recognition through self-representation is a microcosm of wider society, as the late-capitalist subject is in constant pursuit of perfection (Holla, 2015).

In this battle of hyper-comparison many individuals outside of appearance-based industries are opting to cosmetically transform and improve the body in a bid to improve job prospects (Hua, 2013; Mears, 2014; Kotzé and Antonopoulos, 2019). This is a trend that can be located within and across culture more widely, especially among young people who are most passionately embracing bodily enhancement (Elliot, 2013). Other consumers also felt that if they could become slimmer, have whiter teeth and generally look more attractive, they would be more likely to progress in their work and social lives. Heather (29), a junior marketing assistant and legitimate beauty consumer, admitted:

> I want to get my teeth whitened. I've been working at the same company for a while now, and I still haven't been promoted. It's because I'm not very confident in delivering presentations and that's big in this industry. I'm so insecure about my teeth and I know if I got them whitened, I would be able to present with confidence and finally progress in my career.

The following account from Grace also illustrates the links that consumers made between employment, success and appearance.

Grace was studying marketing at university and regularly attended the (counterfeit) Botox parties as part of the Clique. She was a consumer of various counterfeit and non-counterfeit make-up products and clothing items from social media sellers. On leaving university, Grace intended to obtain a well-paid job. However, as she became aware that a university degree in Britain no longer guaranteed this (Brown and Hesketh, 2004), she had begun to consider her appearance as a way to provide herself with an edge in the job market:

> Although knowledge is important, a good degree doesn't exactly guarantee a well-paid job anymore … although it's never acknowledged, employers most certainly judge a person based on their appearance. In this day and age, beauty is key. If you're good looking you have more chance of getting a job … I know university will go so quickly so I'll really focus on improving and taking care of my appearance. Hopefully, then I'll bag myself my dream job.

Although educational qualifications and work experience are important, in a consumer society fixated on appearance workplace success is increasingly associated with image, self-marketing and beauty (Elliot, 2013). Indeed, many of the participants held the belief that if they were to increase their bodily capital and invest in their consumer lifestyle that they would subsequently be able to improve their friendships, their popularity and secure further employment opportunities in both licit and illicit markets. Similarly, male participants in Kotzé and Antonopoulos's (2019) ethnographic study understood the importance of achieving an aesthetically pleasing and instrumentally effective body to increase 'bodily capital' and successfully do their job. Therefore, beauty products and procedures are used as a means of hyper-conforming to commodified gender norms and the neoliberal tenets driving consumer capitalism.

The symbolic value of (counterfeit) beauty brands

Consistent with existing findings on the consumption and supply of fashion counterfeits (Treadwell, 2011; Large, 2019; Bardey et al, 2022), the participants were turning to the internet to buy (counterfeit and non-counterfeit) beauty products. To give a handful of examples, Jessica bought a range of branded counterfeit make-up, perfume and clothing items from social media sellers across various platforms. Ryan bought (counterfeit and non-counterfeit) aftershave products from Facebook sellers. Grace, Lauren and Olivia all bought various counterfeit and non-counterfeit make-up products and clothing items from social media sellers on Instagram and Facebook. Sophie and Carys also reflected on their experiences of buying counterfeit teeth whitening kits online from retail websites.

Although most consumers intentionally sought out counterfeits primarily because of their low cost, it was not uncommon for consumers to be deceived into buying counterfeits. Issues of deception and quality surrounding any product are exacerbated when the purchase occurs online (Treadwell, 2011; Large, 2019), especially in the case of beauty products which can cause physical damage to the consumer (Roberton, 2017). Yet, somewhat paradoxically, being deceived played a fundamental role in Jessica's decision to continue buying counterfeits. Despite working in a low-wage job as a waitress, Jessica actively rejected buying beauty and fashion goods without a luxury, recognizable brand name. She understood the symbolic value of buying particular brands and took a great deal of pride in the brands she associated herself with. Seeking to reduce her outgoing expenses without compromising on the value of the brand, Jessica recalled a time when she sought a cheaper deal online:

> I saw my foundation on eBay for around 40 per cent off. I didn't realize it was a fake until it arrived. The bottle looked pretty much the same, but the quality wasn't as good. You see so much in the news about

> people having allergic reactions from fakes, but I had no problems with it … It made me completely change my view on fakes. I thought fakes were tacky and dangerous, but now I actively search online for them. I love a bargain. If anything, that eBay seller did me a huge favour. I save so much money, and I've upgraded to better brands than I previously bought.

Jessica's account illustrates how the internet can enable consumers to displace their concerns about counterfeits or harm. When I met Jessica she had been buying counterfeit beauty products for over a year but she had never used cosmetic enhancement drugs. However, it was during my fieldwork that, influenced by her friends, she began to use counterfeit facial injectables at the Botox parties discussed earlier. Driven by her desire to continue consuming 'branded' products in a more financially viable manner, she was willing to overlook the authenticity of a product or service and the associated reductions in quality. The possibilities for harm were seen as something external to her experiences and were, to her mind, a minimal risk she was willing to take. For Jessica, the symbolic value of buying into a brand superseded any concerns of the authenticity of the product. In this regard, consuming brands, counterfeit or not, are used as a symbolic communicator for individualistic distinction from the masses of consumers.

> It was a Thursday evening in mid-May and Jessica wanted to go out to a popular bar just outside of Beaufort. We managed to get seats in the main seating area and, after a few drinks, Jessica reached into her Mulberry handbag and pulled out a smaller Dior make-up bag. She placed it on the table next to her glass of Sauvignon Blanc and smiled. She then unzipped the bag with a distinct air of excitement and told me to look inside it. As I rummaged through the bag, I noticed Jessica gazing around the room to see if anyone acknowledged her and her luxurious make-up bag. Everything in the bag looked expensive. It was pretty clear these products were not the standard high-street brands you could buy in your local Superdrug: Chanel perfume, an unopened bottle of Estée Lauder foundation, and a range of other products from the likes of Charlotte Tilbury, Bobbi Brown and Yves Saint Laurent. With a massive grin on her face, she continued to look around the room and began spraying herself with the Chanel perfume. My phone suddenly buzzed. A text message from Jessica read: 'It's all fake!' The entire contents of her make-up bag came from various Facebook sellers, costing her approximately £80. The following day Jessica coyly admitted that showing me the entire contents of her make-up bag in the middle of a busy bar was a calculated tactic to display her high-end branded products, which evidenced success. She was endeavouring to inspire envy in others. (fieldnote)

Jessica demonstrated an interesting blend of perceived 'savviness' mixed with conspicuous consumption. Such willingness to portray herself as successful is thinly veiled in the sense that she was eager to acknowledge that the products were fake because of how much money she saved. Whether the product was counterfeit or authentic did not appear to be a concern as the 'representation' of the brand was of higher importance. This mindset was not unique to Jessica. Ryan worked as a car salesman and took great pride in having a well-groomed appearance. While he did not go out of his way to buy counterfeits, he often bought (counterfeit and non-counterfeit) items from Facebook Marketplace. Ryan explained, 'If it's like the real thing then I'm happy to buy it, real or not'. This approach resonates with one participant from Large's (2019) research, where the symbolic value of buying into a brand appeared to be more important than whether the product was produced by that brand. Indeed, as the boundaries between the 'real' and the 'representation' are becoming increasingly blurred, the consumption of counterfeits can serve as a status symbol in the same way as non-counterfeit branded goods (Veblen, 2005).

Other consumers who had bought counterfeits online were aware that they were, or could be, counterfeit. With the huge growth in 'fast fashion' and the intertwined phenomenon of 'fast beauty', consumer perceptions towards shopping for affordable trends have changed. In many ways, Primark and Shein are emblematic of this, as consumers buy new fashion and beauty items despite the well-known ethical concerns and environmental issues associated with the supply chain (see Crewe, 2017; Large, 2019). In fact, consumers are now becoming increasingly proud to obtain a good deal on the desired product and are no longer embarrassed to trade down (Yurchisin and Johnson, 2010; Bardey et al, 2022) if the product looks of greater value than it costs. An example of this can be seen with the rise of social media users creating clothing and beauty 'haul videos' that showcase their latest purchases and bargains. However, trading down to a cheaper brand was not always desirable, especially if the brand had negative connotations for identity. Jessica comments:

> The brands you buy pretty much define who you are … No one buys make-up from brands like Rimmel anymore. It's just not cool. It's so important to keep up appearances and be as good as everyone else. No one knows the difference [between the counterfeit and non-counterfeit products], so I don't see any harm in it.

Prior to buying a brand, the consumer is expected to understand what the brand represents, the meaning and lifestyle associated with the brand and the exchange value of consuming the brand. In a society where representation has supplanted reality, and conspicuous consumption of luxury products dominates the construction of the self, appearance has become what Featherstone (2010: 200) describes as a 'work of art'.

Jessica, Ryan and many other consumers across the research bought counterfeit branded products that equated to their identities of 'cool individualism' (Hall, 2012a) which were more distinct than others who bought 'cheap' value brands. They understood the symbolic value of buying counterfeit versions of luxury brands (for example, Chanel) and believed them to be greater than non-counterfeit brands (for example, Rimmel) because of the meaning, value and lifestyle associated with that certain brand. This was based on the notion that products are defined by what they signify, rather than their use of authenticity (Baudrillard, 1998). When asked about the risks associated with using fake products, they appeared to only consider the potential physical harm of skin irritation from beauty products and thought this comparable to the same risks from legitimate products.

With the exception of David, the participants understood that for them to socially survive, they had to keep abreast of the cultural meaning attached to consumer items and be reflexive enough to distance themselves from items as trends changed (Winlow and Hall, 2006). Exemplifying this, Ryan shed light upon a time where he had to distance himself from certain brands that were no longer 'cool', despite liking them:

> When I was younger, I would just spray some Lynx on and put a bit of gel in my hair. I wouldn't be seen dead wearing Lynx now. It's cheap, childish and just not cool … I then moved on to brands like David Beckham and Lacoste, the really cheap ones you can get on the high-street for under twenty pounds. They don't smell bad but no one this age wears that. If someone asks you what you're wearing you've got to be able to tell them something good and not 'I'm wearing David Beckham' … I'm all about Armani now.

As the meaning of brands and specific forms of consumer items are in flux, young people are expected to stay up to date and conversant with the contextual meanings of the latest trends and fads. At the same time, the over-abundance of beauty and fashion brands and the prospective range of choices on offer were contributing to the anxiety and insecurity that seemingly permeated all aspects of the lives of the participants. Often, they were expected to 'take a chance and guess' (Elle) as to whether their choice of brand and product would pay off. They were constantly caught up in a viscous cycle of desire and dissatisfaction, as Grace explained:

> I feel like I'm always late buying something, and by the time I have it, it's no longer cool. I remember when everyone got hyped over Michael Kors watches. I wanted one so badly, but I couldn't afford it.

> My parents got me one for my birthday. I was so happy and excited when I opened it. It sounds stupid but it was like I could fit in again, all my friends at the time had them. But I only wore it once. They weren't cool anymore because everyone had them. Even people online will call you a basic bitch if you upload a picture wearing one … You have to associate yourself with the right brands and styles.

Grace described the intense sense of pressure to make the right choice. As Bauman (2001: 25) notes, 'the consumer market offers choice complete with the reassurance that the choice is right'. Those who fail to make the right choices become at risk of falling into the category of 'flawed consumers' (Bauman, 2005: 25), negatively labelled (for example, Grace as a 'basic bitch' with her watch) and at risk of becoming a figure of mockery and humiliation (Hall et al, 2008). In the absence of traditional forms of labour structures, distinct value systems and markers of identity, consumerism and commodified leisure increasingly facilitate friendships (for example, the Clique) (Hall and Winlow, 2005; Ayres, 2019). Therefore, as Ayres (2019: 139) remarks, 'such forms of cultural degradation and exile constitute the ultimate form of exclusion, representing a life not lived'. Consumerism is fraught with challenges, harms and dangers; it produces risks and anxieties that unavoidably impact in a corrosive way upon behavioural norms and practices (Winlow and Hall, 2006). With so much emphasis on brands and the pressure for individuals to associate themselves with a particular brand and style that signals success over failure, it is perhaps unsurprising that many young people are engaging in counterfeit consumption to keep up with emerging trends and the ever-increasing pressures to consume, and for such consumption to be successful (Large, 2019)

Furthermore, Grace told me that she 'felt no different' after obtaining the watch. As discussed in Chapter 2, in psychoanalytical terms the foundations of consumerism are rooted not in enjoyment, but in a perpetual sense of dissatisfaction. Dissatisfaction is what the likes of McGowan (2016) suggest consumers find most satisfying. Before Grace acquired the watch, the item held a sublime status, presenting itself as the ultimate object of her desire. Nevertheless, once the watch was acquired, it began to lose its appeal and the cycle of dissatisfaction and desire restarted. This was the reality for most of the participants, where the acquisition of the desired item (or consumer experience) failed to deliver any lasting sense of satisfaction. Satisfaction was fleeting and fuelled further desires to consume newer, better and potentially more harmful products and experiences. For the participants, the consumption of brands was frequently regarded as an essential part of identity construction and, as such, any objects that were not a part of, or congruent with, the brands these individuals associated themselves with would be eschewed, irrespective of any individual liking of these objects.

Other examples of this included Olivia switching from L'Oreal make-up to (counterfeit) Mac make-up; Craig distancing himself from Superdry as the brand was no longer deemed 'cool' by his friends; Sophie upgrading her make-up regime to include NARS products instead of Maybelline.

'We shouldn't have to spend so much to look younger': DIY facial injectables

Throughout my time in the field, it became evident that the physical appearance of the self was a focal point for most of the participants as they enthusiastically disclosed and discussed the various procedures and bodily alterations they had undergone. Olivia was a prime example of this. When we first met, she confidently listed the procedures and surgeries she had completed, along with the ones she wanted to have done in the future: at 18 she had a breast augmentation, by the age of 21 she had undergone rhinoplasty and was seriously considering both Botox and lip filler; by 25 these ideas had become reality, as she had (counterfeit) Botox and dermal fillers in various parts of her face, had her teeth professionally whitened and was now considering getting veneers.

It was clear when speaking with the participants that the symbolic value of buying branded goods was accompanied by an increased emphasis and significance on the perceived aesthetic improvement of their faces and bodies. The consumption and use of beauty was high on the agenda for all of the female participants who wore (high-end and branded) make-up on a daily basis; regularly attended salons for hair, nails, facials and tanning; frequented the gym and took pride in their appearances; and had regular non-invasive cosmetic procedures including Botox, dermal fillers, microdermabrasion, laser hair removal and teeth whitening. These procedures were not always delivered in professional settings, with several of them being administered through DIY kits or in informal gatherings, with limited concern paid to the possibility for harm to occur as a consequence of such administration.

As mentioned in Chapter 4, one of the key ways in which these procedures were delivered was through 'Botox parties', which I was fortunate enough to be invited to as part of my fieldwork. The informal nature of these parties appeared to be a fundamental reason as to why it was so easy for the potentials for harm to be disavowed by the members of the Clique. While they were now all aware of the illicit nature of the products and services they were engaging with, this was not always the case prior to and even during the parties. Olivia reflected on receiving lip filler from Carys:

> I was saving money, and I planned on getting lip filler the year after. I would always tell Reanne that I wanted to get my lips done, and

> she knew I was struggling with money at the time. I went to her house one night for a few drinks with her and her friends. It turned out to be a bit of a Botox party … After a couple of drinks, I ended up getting my lips done. I couldn't believe how cheap it was … They assumed I knew [that the products were counterfeit], but to be honest, I had no problem with it. She did a good job and my lips looked great after.

At the time of this party, Olivia had a full-time position as a model, and because of this was cautious of, and did not want to risk, any activity or procedure that might cause physical damage to her face. She had placed her trust in Carys and the rest of the Clique, and while she was impressed and happy with the outcome of the procedure and now regularly consumes counterfeit Botox and dermal fillers, she explained that if she had known about the illicit status of the products or of Carys's lack of expertise at the time, she would not have undergone the procedure in the first place. In this scenario, the initial consumption of counterfeit products was driven by a level of deception, but as Olivia positively reflected on how cheap such products were in this setting, this was not enough to prevent any future consumption of illicit beauty products. If anything, it had the opposite effect. As the participants had positive experiences and outcomes with these products, their fears over potential risks diminished.

This diminishing concern over risk and disregard for the possible harms accompanying the consumption of such products was repeated across the participants. Instead, they placed an emphasis on both the affordability and the perceived comparability between genuine and counterfeit products. At the same time, there is an increasing accessibility for purchasing facial injectables online (to be discussed later), alongside a rise in social media content and guidance on how to use such products. Combined, such accessibility and availability of product and content is reducing the perceived level of harm inherent in such consumption. It is no surprise then that as the perceived level of risk lessens, and as the exposure to such procedures either in-person or online increases, the use of facial injectables such as Botox and dermal fillers become hyper-normalized within contemporary society (Cook and Dwyer, 2017). Consequently, consumers are turning to such products at ever younger ages as they search for quick fixes that promise to alter their appearance.

Grace was no exception to this as, at the age of 17, she had tried to get lip filler administered at various professional clinics but was turned away as being deemed 'too young' to receive such a procedure. Despite the relatively recent criminalization of these acts,[1] there has been a longstanding belief within the medical profession that providing such procedures to younger people is deeply unethical due to the facial structure still changing and growing as they mature (Save Face, 2019). Unable to find a medical professional willing to perform the procedure, Grace opted for a riskier alternative:

> Carys was my hairdresser, so I knew her before the parties. One day while getting my haircut, she mentioned that she had started doing these little gatherings. I thought they sounded so fun. I had only just turned 17 and thought I would have to wait a year to get work done to my face. I thought everyone would turn me away for being too young. I asked Carys if I could come along to the next one. She checked with Reanne, and around six weeks after, I went to one of the parties … I wasn't worried about [the illicit nature of the parties]. Honestly, I didn't see it as any different from seeing [a professional].

Although there was some awareness among the group of the potential dangers associated with the use of illicit cosmetic injectables, the benefits and rewards of facial enhancement, along with levels of personal trust in those administering the procedures, outweighed and mitigated any concerns over the potential for harm. This view was shared across the group, and, significantly, for many within the group the legal status surrounding the services and products was of minimal concern as they deemed prospective harms between these procedures and legitimate cosmetic enhancements to be equivalent. As Reanne elucidates:

> I know people care about training and expertise, but I don't. When I first had something done, I knew Carys and trusted her. She isn't the type of person who would do something that could cause someone harm. Yeah, there are risks with everything, but I don't see the risks as being any higher than going to a so-called professional. This way we get to do it at my house and make a real night of it … You have to take risks to look good.

Such a view was also shared with Elle, who commented on her first Botox party:

> I knew what was on offer. I had seen Reanne's results from Carys, and she always looked great. I went along to find out a bit more about it all. I was thinking about getting Botox for a while anyway, but the thought of being injected always put me off. After a few drinks I ended up getting Botox that night, and that's when I met the other girls. We are all pretty much inseparable now. I've never had friends like them before.

As discussed, the motivations and perceptions of the riskiness of these procedures was mitigated and mediated by individual levels of trust and the positioning of professional services as just as risky as procedures delivered at home, minus the comfort and convenience that delivery in a domestic setting provides.

Such motivations were similarly articulated by consumers in beauty-related forums and Facebook groups which, along with aesthetic concerns over ageing and the peer pressure associated with idealized body images, would frequently invoke the need to reduce the financial costs associated with professional procedures as clear motivators for engaging with DIY procedures:

> The salons are too expensive. It's a lot easier and cheaper to DIY. The last time I had it done professionally, it didn't even look good or last very long … Since finding a good deal online, I won't ever go back. It's so easy to inject, and my skin looks like I've been airbrushed. (Comment in closed Facebook group)

Furthermore:

> We shouldn't have to spend so much to look younger. In my opinion, it's not worth going to a clinic. DIY is so much cheaper, and you can just easily top it up as and when you need. It's not hard to do. Just watch a couple of YouTube videos. There are so many out there. (Comment in a closed Facebook group)

The lack of convenience and disappointment with the outcomes of services administered by professionals was a continual source of frustration for consumers engaging with one another within these online spaces and served as a clear rationale for consumers wanting to take control of their beauty regimes and order products online for self-injection (Hall and Antonopoulos, 2016). These spaces also served as information sharing spaces as recommendations for websites and online sellers were often circulated on various discussion threads, with users offering one another advice when ordering the products, sharing their experiences of sellers and advising one another to use YouTube videos to educate themselves before injecting. It is clear then that pursuits of perfecting the face and body through undergoing cosmetic enhancements are driven by a range of motivations that extend beyond simply wanting to 'look good'. The presence and visibility of products and procedures online is hyper-normalizing their everydayness and reducing barriers and fears over the administering of DIY injectables. When access or costs with professional services are deemed too high, when the quality of such services is deemed to be lacking, and when there are equivalences made between the associated risks of products administered in professional settings compared with domestic setting, then it is no wonder that consumers are turning to cost-effective procedures to meet their needs.

Blurring the boundaries between 'health' and 'enhancement'

In the same way as beauty and fitness regimes, young people are self-managing their healthcare regimes for cosmetic and aesthetic purposes. The participants often spoke of how they were attempting to look 'healthy' through unnatural enhancement products, which the internet increasingly enabled and exploited (see Hall and Antonopoulos, 2016). For example, Liam regularly bought weight-loss drugs from an online pharmacy (OP), but when he made his first online order, he thought the website was legitimate. When he received the order, he became more suspicious over the legitimacy of the products and OP as the products were shipped from Hong Kong. Liam checked whether the OP was legitimate on 'LegitScript.com' – a website that was recommended to him via a forum website for weight loss – which identified the website as a 'rogue pharmacy'. Despite being aware that the website was not necessarily legitimate, Liam showed no concern over the illicit nature of the product and subsequently re-purchased it. Many of these websites accepted payments via electronic payment methods (for example, credit card and PayPal), while some platforms encouraged direct transfers between bank accounts by offering a discount (usually between 5–10 per cent) for customers who opted for that method. Certain websites offered 'discount schemes', where the larger the order value, the larger the discount, and others included promotional offers on bulk purchases of specific products.

Alongside purchasing products from OPs, Liam used online participatory spaces (forums and Facebook groups) to source products for weight-loss and attain advice and experiences from those who occupy these diet cultures. Virtual spaces are often utilized by many individuals as a 'positive space full of good vibes to share your journey, get tips and come for support' (as one of the [closed] Facebook weight-loss and fitness-support groups described itself). These types of groups were often full of hashtag trends (for example, 'Fitspiration'), a constant flow of transformation photos and images of meals. The shared experiences offered by these types of groups played a predominant factor in Liam's purchase of weight-loss drugs. He emphasized the discomfort he had previously felt at dieting groups such as Slimming World, and how the digital and distanced nature of online spaces provided him with a degree of anonymity that ensured he would avoid the feelings of humiliation that he had previously experienced. Therefore, as Fox et al (2005) note, the internet enables consumers to access products, information and support to self-govern their healthcare regimes. Such accessibility of information is contributing to contemporary trends in 'prosumption' (Beer and Burrows, 2010), further blurring the boundaries between 'health' and 'enhancement' and between the 'patient' and 'consumer' (Hall, 2019).

Additionally, the internet promotes mainstream and generalized constructions of body size, shape and health. Not only does this leave consumers open to greater risks associated with diet cultures and weight-loss products as they strive to achieve particular unhealthy constructions of the body, but it also offers numerous opportunities for personal and social harm. Despite the potentially liberating role of consumption, many consumers spoke of weight-loss products, fad diets and exercise regimes as a result of the constant pressure to conform to current trends and overcome their body dissatisfaction. As such, online participatory spaces further perpetuate and intensify an endless loop of hyper-comparison through the promotion of physical enhancement and improvement practices. In this sense, it is not surprising that young people opt for a quick fix approach to alter their appearance, especially as body image is seen as being central to self-esteem (Fedorak, 2017).

Hyper-conforming to cultural norms

Motivations for enhancing the body appeared to go beyond labour markets, and consumers often prioritized short-term aesthetic gratification over long-term health. This was emblematic of the capitalist injunction to acquire the commodified masculine or feminine ideal to physically advance the self above others and gain immediate gratification. The women within this study were constantly attempting to look like what they thought women should look like, and the men were constantly attempting to look like what they thought men should look like. The experiences of Liam exemplified this. Liam used exercise, dieting and weight-loss drugs to increase his self-worth, bodily capital and mental wellbeing by hyper-conforming to commodified gender norms and the cultural values of neoliberalism. Liam had struggled with his weight and body image for his whole life. He had tried an abundance of diets and exercise regimes to lose weight but found them extremely difficult to uphold. When I first met Liam, he was attempting to follow a ketogenic diet, a very low-carbohydrate, high-fat diet:

> I've done the 5:2 diet, Weight Watchers, Slimming World, the Body Coach plan, Insanity, and I've had a PT [personal trainer] before. Nothing seems to work long-term. I lose a bit of weight, but it's so hard to be consistent with it. Especially as my whole university life involved going out, drinking a lot, and then eating calorific food when I'm hungover … When you attend those diet groups, like Slimming World, they weigh you. It can be humiliating if you haven't lost anything … [pause] it just makes you feel like a failure, especially if you've tried hard that week and stayed on plan. It becomes too much, and you give up, go off the rails and eat whatever. I'm still trying to

> lose weight, but I've given up on those types of diets now. I feel so shit after because I waste so much time and money for nothing … I'm so tired of measuring my self-worth based on the number on the scales. But I know if I lose weight, I will be more confident in life.

Aged 18, Liam left school, and after failing to get the correct grades for his chosen university, he spent a couple of years working at a supermarket in his hometown in the Midlands. Liam re-applied for university in his early twenties and completed an undergraduate degree in politics and economics. He then relocated to a commuter town just outside of London to fulfil a role in what he deemed as the 'dream job'. He moved into rented accommodation with two friends who had also made the journey down south after graduating. Shortly after our first meeting, Liam was made redundant due to his employer needing to cut costs and reduce staff numbers. Unwilling to compromise on the type of jobs he was applying for, Liam soon found himself marginalized and unable to access the circuits of consumer culture which he was accustomed to during his time working in the city. Longing for a 'career, not a job', Liam would only apply for jobs suited to his degree:

> I liked where I worked. It made me feel worth something, and it gave me a purpose. People would ask what I do for a living, and it was who I was, it was my identity. It was like I finally belonged somewhere, and I wasn't just fat [Liam]. I was [Liam] with a career in London. I was doing something worthwhile. Now I'm just like, who the fuck am I? It's 2 pm on a Monday, and I'm sitting in the pub, unemployed … I don't want to move back home, but I'm also not going to apply for any old job. I need to sort myself out. My confidence has hit an all-time low.

Liam differed from the other participants as, for him, work was not something which had to be endured; work provided Liam with a sense of social status and distinction. Losing his job was detrimental to his self-confidence and after a short period of self-loathing, losing weight became a feasible way for him to retain an element of control over his life (Kotzé and Antonopoulos, 2019).

Three weeks later we met at a pub near his home. At first glance, I barely recognized him: he was wearing a suit, he had lost a lot of weight, and his hair was shorter. With a beer in hand, Liam told me that he had just come from a job interview for a big company in London. He then proceeded to tell me how he had spent the last couple of weeks turning his life around:

> [Over the last six months] I've been to more job interviews than I've had hot dinners. But I think this is the one. They seemed to like me … I've spent quite a bit of money lately, just trying to turn my life around

> and better myself. I've lost around 1.5 stone. I was just so fed up with feeling rubbish, dieting, and then feeling worse for failing. I started talking to some people online, in one of those weight-loss groups on Facebook. Someone recommended some pills to help. I wasn't sure at first, but I couldn't continue how I was. I've been trying to lose weight for years. I've got a long way to go, but it's a step in the right direction. For the first time in forever, I feel good. And I haven't had to step inside a gym. I've cleaned my diet up a bit, but I still drink lots of this [he holds his beer up high]. These pills are magic [laughs].

He looked proud. I was unsure how he was surviving, as the last time I had seen him he had no money whatsoever; and he had been unemployed for six months at this point. Rather than succumb to the cultural insignificance that was signified by being unable to maintain a presence within the circuits of consumption, Liam had taken out a loan to help pay his bills and rent and finance his new lifestyle. He repeatedly said: 'It's an investment!' Despite trying an abundance of diet and fitness programmes, Liam never achieved the results he desired; daily practices of self-management were seen as an imposition for him. The anticipation of failure associated with dieting was a negative experience for Liam. The dieting industry creates a problem of body dissatisfaction and then exploits this problem and offers a commercialized solution to overcome it. As Ogden (1992: 48) remarks, 'by creating a market for itself it ensures that women [and men] will continue to feel fat and will continue to support the dieting industry'.

The term 'dieting' has different meanings for different people, and approaches to it differ in numerous ways: from reducing the intake of calories; following programmes such as Slim Fast and Juice Plus, where meals are replaced with low-calorie drinks; following controlled programmes such as Slimming World and Weight Watchers; to more extreme strategies for weight loss that include laxative use, vomiting, weight-loss drugs and fad diets. The ability to modify the body through a range of commercialized regimes and technologies can be used to construct the desired appearance, or in most cases attempt to construct an unrealistic beauty ideal. Of course, these methods can all be particularly dangerous, especially when used by normal-weight individuals who perceive themselves as being overweight, leading to negative health impacts and even deaths (McKay, 2020). However, for Liam, the idea that he could 'finally' lose weight without having to spend time in the gym or sign up for another diet appeared to overshadow any real concern for risk and harm. Liam's willingness to use illicit weight-loss drugs to achieve an appropriately slim body and provide himself with immediate gratification, irrespective of the potentially damaging physical and psychological impact, highlights the extent young people will go to acquire the 'correct' physique and reclaim a form of control over their fluid lives.

Liam's remarks resonate with one of Kotzé and Antonopoulos's (2019: 690) participants, Moe, who claimed to have 'no college, no job, no girlfriend' and used steroids as a way to seize control over his life and obtain a hyper-masculine body. Magazines, TV shows, the internet and advertisements all portray an increasingly masculine body that is becoming unattainable for the majority of men, as the feminine ideal is for women (Dittmar and Halliwell, 2008). Male bodies that have been commercialized and celebrated within the bodybuilding community, along with the surrounding consumer culture, often embody typical idealized body types that are masculine, lean, strong and tanned. For instance, depictions of the hyper-masculine image through action figures, video games, films, comic books and television has increasingly come to glorify unrealistic standards of a physique that is unobtainable by natural means (Dunne et al, 2006). This can drive some men to use steroids to acquire the standards of muscularity proffered by hyper-masculine images (Walker and Joubert, 2011; Kotzé and Antonopoulos, 2019) or, in the case for some of Brandon's customers, use melanotan II (M2) products to create the illusion of the desired aesthetic. At bodybuilding competitions, competitors have long used tanning products as a way to increase muscle definition on the stage as muscles appear more prominent on tanned skin (Monaghan, 2001). Although there are many ways in which ideal femininity and hegemonic masculinity are challenged in bodybuilding, and many female bodybuilders attempt to accentuate their muscular development, appreciating both their appearance and physical strength (see Mulrooney and van de Ven, 2019), it appeared that there was a relationship between men on the quest to self-improvement and the pressures to conform to the idealized bodybuilding physique. For instance, Brandon's customers within the gym environment were openly using M2 products to obtain this goal. This is just one example of how fitness can go beyond 'healthy', where the body becomes a site of contemporary consumption for aesthetic reasons rather than health-related matters (Kotzé and Antonopoulos, 2019).

Therefore, as Bauman (2005) notes, often when the body is brought to a state of 'fitness', it contradicts the very purpose that the state was intended to serve. In most cases, fitness is no longer about health and wellbeing or muscular and cardiovascular endurance, it is about the aesthetic composition of the body. As Bauman (2005: 93) remarks, '"fitness" is to a consumer in the society of consumers what "health" was to the producer in the society of producers'. Indeed, the use of M2 products to create the illusion of increased muscle definition was a way of speeding up the process of aesthetically priming and refining the body. Arguably, the use of such products to physically advance the self above others is, therefore, concomitant of the neoliberal risk-taking ethic (Kindynis, 2016), as these consumers were showing the attitudes, norms, values, drives and desires coveted by market capitalism (Kotzé and Antonopoulos, 2019). Indeed, several studies indicate that the use of performance and image enhancing drugs (PIEDs) is often not seen as a sign of deviant or transgressive behaviour but something that is a necessary part of bodybuilding, such as training and nutrition (Monaghan, 2001; Keane, 2005). It is also important to reiterate that these men were not professional or competitive bodybuilders. Therefore, the use of risky beauty products may be related to the sense of belonging to a social group and hyper-comparison among the fitness community, as opposed to bodybuilding more specifically.

This alteration of the body in order to foster a sense of belonging was not something that was exclusively the domain of such communities. The same logics and motivations as discussed earlier were also found in Sophie, who, like many others, viewed her appearance as the only thing she had a degree of control over. Before she worked as an eyelash technician, Sophie had attempted to go to university but found studying too challenging and returned to her hometown before the end of the first semester. When she talked about her early departure from university she coyly admitted to feeling like a 'failure' and experienced a period of shame and embarrassment. Following her short-lived experience at university, Sophie found it extremely difficult to find a job that offered her the satisfaction and fulfilment she desired. She decided to enrol on a course in eyelash extensions in the hope of becoming a self-employed eyelash technician. Sophie described herself as being 'lazy' and 'overweight' during her late teens and early twenties. But at the age of 21 she decided to lose weight and embark on a healthier lifestyle. She believed losing weight would guarantee her happiness, satisfaction and enable her to regain some form of control over her life:

> I was around three stone heavier than I am now. I was a university drop out and just felt so lost in life. Since losing weight I've transformed into a completely different person. I never knew I could feel so confident. It has made me feel a lot happier. I was in a pretty dark place back then, and I felt like I had zero control over anything in my life.

Just like Liam, Sophie's experiences of lacking direction and feeling like a failure manifested in her dissatisfaction with her own body, which became the primary focus of her efforts to turn her life around. Whether through natural or unnatural methods, the idea that appearance was the only thing many consumers could control is reflective of broader socio-economic issues (Kotzé and Antonopoulos, 2019). While Sophie, Liam and many others contend that they are exercising individual choice and retaining some control over their lives through making their own decisions and choices, they are ultimately hyper-conforming to what is now a heavily commodified ideal of femininity and masculinity. Against this backdrop, it is perhaps unsurprising that there exists a booming demand for body-altering products and a willingness to inflict harm.

Chapter summary

In the absence of fulfilling and meaningful employment opportunities, it is not surprising that there exists a booming demand for beauty and body-altering products. Building upon Chapter 4, this chapter has documented how consuming and supplying illicit goods and services is both conformist and an integral part of surviving within the contemporary landscape of consumer capitalism. Beauty is very much a tool for the late-capitalist worker-consumer, fulfilling a range of everyday functions. These include the enhancement of the face and body; improving social standing and leisure experiences; facilitating and maintaining friendships; increasing the chance of securing a job or further work; and regaining a sense of control over their everyday lives. In a competitive consumer culture characterized by hyper-comparison, hyper-consumption and competitive individualism, and filled with pressures and insecurities about appearances, work and general life, some young people are using quick-fix beauty and healthcare products that promise to assuage anxieties. This chapter has offered an insight into beauty consumption and beauty identities to demonstrate how beauty is capital in contemporary society and how looking good is now considered as a way to improve both social and working lives.

6

From Filters to Fillers: The Real-Life Instagram Face

Introduction

Having explored the instrumental motivations of (counterfeit) beauty consumption, this chapter sets out to examine the role of hyper-comparison in online spaces and real life, including the impact it has upon human subjectivities and young people's willingness to engage in harmful acts. The use of social media has distorted ideas and views on what is natural, unnatural, realistic and unrealistic. Indeed, the development of this form of hyper-comparison is inextricably bound up with the cultural changes and technological advances taking place across the landscape of late capitalism, which have placed notions of narcissism, competitive individualism and profound insecurity at the centre of contemporary existence (Hall et al, 2008; Ayres, 2020). This chapter will paint a picture of what has driven the research participants to have these distorted views and the impact this is having on their lives.

Distorted views: young people's objective reality

The proliferation of social media has facilitated and enabled a global, real-time connectivity and engagement with friends and peers that would have been hard to imagine at the turn of the twenty-first century. This ever-present digital connectivity through networked devices has radically changed the nature of social interactions and the ways in which people spend their everyday lives. Besides David, all the participants were active on social media throughout the fieldwork and spent numerous hours a day on social media platforms. They would often sit next to their friends, endlessly scrolling through their social media newsfeeds, replying to messages and liking photos. They were interacting all day, but almost entirely through a screen. This undeniably impacted the ways in which they viewed the world.

While social media platforms enable people to connect and interact with others, regardless of the time of day or geographical location, spending an increased amount of time on social media comes with hyper-comparison, aggressive presentation of the idealized self, the sense of feeling behind in life, not being good enough and the fear of missing out (FOMO) (Irwin-Rogers, 2019). It is this opportunity for self-expression provided by consumer markets that has innumerable effects that appear to negatively impact mental health (James, 2010; Cederström and Spicer, 2015). This has led to some referring to social media as 'antisocial media' (Wood, 2016) due to its potentially harmful effect on social relations and its role in the ongoing crisis among young people's mental health in recent years (Royal Society for Public Health, 2017).

Given the increasing presence of social media use in everyday life, it was perhaps to be expected that this democratization of photo-editing tools and filters would affect the self-esteem of social media users. In many ways, social media puts a lot of the individual and social issues faced by young people under a magnifying glass, enlarging their problems, flaws and insecurities and demanding constant inspection of the self, of others and the world. Such emphasis on the use of social media as a prism through which identity is played, performed and constructed is contributing to the warping of self-perception that drives the liquid modern individual's search for belonging and meaning in a society dominated by consumer ideology (Bauman, 2000). As the following account of Elle and Jessica on a night out in the city demonstrates, constant exposure to the lives of others, particularly within the heavily filtered Instagram world, can significantly impact a young person's sense of objective reality.

> It was a Wednesday evening in the middle of summer, and I met Elle and Jessica in the city. They had spoken about coming to this particular bar for weeks to take some new photos for Instagram; it was a popular location for many social media users. We arrived at the bar and were greeted at the front door by a member of staff who promptly directed us to our table. It was a sophisticated yet modish setting. From the deep red walls and large hanging mirrors to the glass chandelier that hung over the wooden tables, the bar was beyond captivating. We sat at the table, and Elle was alarmingly subdued compared to her usual talkative self. After our 'Instagram-worthy' cocktails had arrived and were photographed, Elle admitted that the bar's interior had made her feel uncomfortable and self-conscious. (fieldnote)

Elle revealed:

> I usually love looking in the mirror, but this is a bit much isn't it? I'm trying to enjoy the night, but I'm just sitting here criticizing my

> reflection. I didn't realize how big the bags under my eyes were. And I thought this top looked good, but it's not flattering at all. I look like I'm six months pregnant ... The longer I look in the mirror, the more I hate my appearance. I spent so much time trying to look nice. I look far from it ... I want to look like I belong on *Love Island*, not ugly island.

Elle took significant pride in her appearance. She had undergone various cosmetic surgeries and regularly attended the (counterfeit) Botox parties as part of the 'Clique', a female friendship group of beauty consumers. Her account of mirror gazing highlights the ways in which a person assesses whether they look 'good' or not and judge whether they are 'beautiful' or not. Confronted by her reflection, Elle became deeply uncomfortable and her account was emblematic of the constant anxiety surrounding our appearance and the flaws we often perceive in ourselves. This disconnection between the perception of oneself and the reality of oneself is in part driven by the blurring of fact and fiction that both social media and traditional media provide their audiences with, transforming reality into a 'hyperreality' (Baudrillard, 1983). As such, young women often conform to what women *should look like* and young men often conform to what men *should look like*. Identity has, thus, become indelibly linked to concepts of excess and commodified images appeared to be far more important than reality itself.

Elle's comparison of herself to contestants on reality television programmes that transform people into celebrities based entirely on their looks and lifestyle, demonstrates how within a hyper-comparative environment the digital landscape has indelibly encouraged young people to emulate such presentations of celebrity. According to the Mental Health Foundation (2021), one in four 18–24 year olds admitted that reality television programmes such as *Love Island* make them worry about how they look. This is perhaps not surprising given that to be a *Love Island* contestant and get selected for the show, individuals need to have the ideal physique. Contestants advance through the series at the expense of others, with their aggressively enhanced appearance often being a core feature of their success. From breast enlargements, rhinoplasty surgeries to veneers and cosmetic injectables, the contestants occupy a specific culture within society and represent a specific body and face type – the gym-honed and often cosmetically enhanced person. Elle's comment that she wanted to look like she was on '*Love Island*, not ugly island' demonstrates how reality television produces unrealistic standards of 'ideal beauty' and shapes ideas about beauty, cosmetic procedures and weight management (Hua, 2013).

Elle's mental construction of the 'perfect body image', produced by her engagement with traditional and social media, affected her perception of her own physical appearance. She was experiencing a deep dissatisfaction that she believed should have been alleviated through her consumer choices. However, this experience was one cultivated by consumer capitalism and its failures to meet its promises and alleviate the anxieties it generates (McGowan, 2016). Following on from Elle's comment, Jessica voiced how Western beauty standards have negatively impacted her perception of herself, making her feel like she was not good enough:

> I've started watching a lot of reality TV and spend far too much time scrolling through social media. And I agree [with Elle], it does make you want to change a lot about your appearance. I've never really considered myself to be fat, not until recently. TV and Instagram constantly bombard you with images of slim and toned people. It just made me realize how out of shape I am. [Jessica pulled out her phone and showed us a photo of a petite, tanned and toned woman on Instagram]. Look at her. She looks so perfect. I've started trying to follow people like that as my motivation.

A continuing theme running through the fieldwork was that young people are now relentlessly incited to surveil the bodies and faces of others. The comparisons Elle and Jessica made with idealized images of beauty resulted in a greater dissatisfaction with their own body image. Within media such as magazines, television programmes, social media and advertisements relating to body image and appearance, individuals are constantly criticized for the way they look. Magazines are renowned for using a magnifying lens and adding red circles to candid images of celebrities to highlight and draw attention to aesthetic 'transgressions' (Elias et al, 2017). Images scrutinizing body shapes, cellulite, teeth, wrinkles, un-depilated hair and skin blemishes have promulgated a certain image of what constitutes the 'perfect body'. As Hall (2019: 178) argues, this has had a 'formative effect on subjectivity' where participants' 'desires, values, beliefs and feelings' were all 'grounded on the common subjective feeling of lack and inferiority that capitalism intensifies and exploits'. As a result, these young people had distorted ideas and views on what was considered natural and unnatural, realistic and unrealistic, and normal and abnormal. These changing ideals and views on what are considered normal and healthy are creating situations in which young people find it increasingly difficult to relate to an external, objective world.

This can be seen in the process of 'life stage dissolution' (Hayward, 2012). As childhood and adulthood are beginning to merge (Smith, 2014), distinct life stages are 'melding into a single undifferentiated consumerist form' (Hall et al, 2008: 201). Grace was a clear example of this, given her use of cosmetic enhancements from the age of 17. With so much pressure to have pixel-perfect skin, young people are injecting potentially harmful amounts of Botox and dermal fillers into the face to emulate their curated digital representation (Hall, 2019). It is hardly surprising that so many of the young people in this study were taking preventative measures earlier, where youth is being extended before it has even finished and faces that are still developing and maturing are being injected with enhancement drugs. However, facial injectables only provide temporary results and often need to be continually topped up to maintain the effects of a wrinkle free, enhanced appearance. By targeting younger populations, the beauty industry is creating consumers that will enlist in a lifetime of beauty and cosmetic enhancement maintenance (Berkowitz, 2017). In this context, we can see how the culture of bodily enhancement and beauty use has emerged and why many of the young people in this study were willing to use potentially dangerous products to change their appearances. Unrealistic beauty standards are harming young people, and the desirable cosmetically enhanced body in real and virtual spaces drives an individual beyond pleasure into the painful realm of jouissance (Žižek, 2002).[1] This growing obsession with self-image and the desire to change the face and body to look more attractive, perform better and be more productive in daily life is leading to a vast amount of psychological harm (Fisher, 2009; Hall, 2019). This can be seen as a microcosm of the broader and more pervasive competitive individualism found in neoliberal society in which young adults are all competitors in the job market (Lloyd, 2013, 2018) and in the night-time economy (NTE) and within circuits of consumption more generally (Hall and Winlow, 2005; Ayres, 2019; Nicholls, 2019).

Furthermore, this constant search for 'new' products promising better and faster results has led to new markets opening up that are potentially more harmful and could have larger detrimental impacts on the physical and mental health of individuals. The participants were constantly seeking the next new thing to help them achieve their goals, and one clear example of this was found in the burgeoning market for diet plans and fitness regimes. As documented in Chapter 5, Liam tried an abundance of commodified diet plans and fitness regimes to attain an ideal physique, resulting in an absence of satisfaction. This dissatisfaction fuelled a further desire to consume weight-loss drugs that he purchased from an online pharmacy (OP). A couple of months after using weight-loss drugs, Liam moved back to his family home in the Midlands. He had exhausted all available avenues of consumer credit and felt that he needed to return home to start paying:

> I got caught up in the city life, and it wasn't healthy for me. The [weight-loss drugs] started to mess with me a bit. I thought they would fix everything, but they didn't. They made me feel more confident for a while, and then I just hit rock bottom and started getting rashes on my skin. I still had no job and couldn't find a job worth staying in London for, but I was in denial. Although I lost a lot of weight, I didn't

> feel good or healthy. I wasted all my money, and it felt like any future prospects like a house were just out of sight … I put the weight all back on again, but now I'm motivated to lose it more healthily and sustainably.

Despite conforming to cultural values of consumerism and self-improvement, he displayed a form of what Stiegler (2013) refers to as a parasuidical disregard for his own life and wellbeing. In these instances of subjective harm, his risk-taking appeared to be undertaken in spite of his knowledge of the potential dangers associated with his behaviour. Shortly after Liam became unemployed, he fell into a state of self-loathing and depressive apathy as he found himself on the 'road to whatever' (Currie, 2005), with a lack of employment opportunities preventing him from securing financial security, stability and happiness. Liam spent a vast amount of time immersed in online participatory forums where the use of weight-loss drugs was somewhat normalized. The drive to distinguish himself within a competitive culture of hyper-comparison led Liam (and many other participants) to resort to drastic measures in which he consumed weight-loss drugs that he had bought online, and which had a detrimental impact on his mental and physical health. Physical harms associated with counterfeit beauty, particularly cosmetic enhancements and pharmaceuticals, were discussed in Chapter 3 and are an area of concern due to the potential dangers they possess for the consumer.

Constructing the real-life Instagram Face

The proliferation of social media apps, the increased levels of engagement and sharing of highly curated content often presents the body and lives of individuals as idealized and perfected, distorting reality and concealing the imperfections and mundanities of everyday life. Such online presentations of the self often serve a dual function: on the one hand, social media acts as a 'digital stage' where users can curate content and present a version of themselves for the outside world; on the other hand, such idealized images also act as a mirror through which the individual comes to understand and control their own identities online. Continual production, exposure and engagement with such curated content, and the appearance apps and filters that often underpin their creation, act as funhouse-mirror reflections of what they should look like, how they should live and who they should be. The contemporary subject now looks at themselves from this point of 'ideal perfection' and compares their 'normal' life and appearance against these ideals, creating the potential for individuals to find their own lives, experiences and appearances as mundane and insufficient. As such, the digitalized body, enhanced by photo-editing apps, is not only creating a one-dimensional beauty ideal, but is also acting as a blueprint for many of the participants' future physical bodies. As the following excerpt from Reanne demonstrates:

> I couldn't help but notice how much filters change the shape of my face for the better. I'd always take selfies through the Snapchat app. It contoured my cheekbones, straightened out my nose and gave more shape to my chin. I looked good … It has made me aware of my imperfections. And made me think, how can I look more like that?

Reanne's emphasis on replicating the online version of herself is telling, as she is aware that she cannot naturally achieve the unrealistic beauty ideals that she is exposed to daily. Instead, solutions were often cheap, quick fixes to accomplish the aspired beauty ideal and meet Western beauty standards. In fact, the most common motivation behind beauty and enhancement products, particularly Botox and dermal filler use, was to look like the technologically mediated images that had been produced online through social media platforms and photo-editing apps. The participants often spoke of how they felt inferior to the unrealistic bodies that are relentlessly displayed online and within the media. I will return to this point in more detail, after drawing on Elle and Sophie, who similarly discussed how digitally altering pictures of themselves made them want to look like these filtered versions. Elle explained:

> I've had lip filler, jaw filler, tear trough filler and a bit of Botox. I've never been overly confident in my skin, but if I'm honest I never thought I'd be the person that would get all this work done by the age of 23. I got to the point where I was editing my pictures to look like everyone else's edited pictures, and I just wanted to look like that full-time. I started with one injection, but over time found myself wanting more and more done. I wanted my face to be more symmetrical like you see in [magazines] and on the TV. Don't get me wrong, I'm happier now, but I could still be a lot happier. I want to change more things about myself.

Elle briefly described how the increased pressures associated with digitally altered images, along with the gradual escalation of what is expected to be normal, motivated her to improve her appearance through cosmetic procedures:

> I went on a Tinder date a while ago. We followed each other on Instagram before the date … When we met, he told me I looked nothing like I do on Instagram. My heart sunk, and it was humiliating. The worst part was, I agreed. I felt like I had catfished him. It was

> around then that I started focusing more on my appearance. I wanted to look more like my pics.

The ability to change and enhance online images and visually improve appearance has blurred the boundaries between the physical and digital presentations of self. An example from Sophie epitomizes the complex nature of having a 'real' and online identity:

> I want to look more like this [Sophie showed me an edited photo of herself]. My cheekbones are more defined, my face looks symmetrical, and my teeth are a perfect shade of white … I'm trying to look more like I do in these pictures. It's sad really, but it is the world we live in. Without social media, people would be less likely to get [cosmetic] work done. But when there are so many different options to change what you hate about yourself, you can use apps to see what you would look like with more enhanced lips or cheekbones or whatever before you get it done. Editing photos is a good way to try before you buy.

Sophie's comments highlight that, whether legitimate or not, the relationship between cosmetic enhancement use and online photo editing has given way to a new phenomenon of the real-life Instagram face. Similar to Reanne and Elle, Sophie used cosmetic enhancements as a way emulate her carefully curated digital representation. The use of modification apps inspired Sophie to use DIY teeth whitening kits and facial injectables at a local aesthetic clinic. Although Sophie paid for her dermal filler procedures, various online retailers offered her free teeth whitening kits in exchange for promotion via a social media post. Sophie never went out of her way to buy counterfeits, but she certainly suspected some of the gifted DIY teeth whitening kits to be counterfeit. Therefore, constant exposure to unrealistic, modified and filtered versions of the self can contribute to the large demand for solutions to overcome feelings of inadequacy.

The growing obsession with self-image and relentless hyper-comparison can exacerbate subjective insecurities and anxieties, affecting overall mental health. Research from the Girlguiding Charity (2020) has shown that 48 per cent of females aged 11–21 years old regularly use apps and filters to improve their online appearance, and 39 per cent reported feeling upset that they did not look like their online versions of themselves in real life. As social media use has increased, mental health issues among young people, and particularly young women, have risen exponentially (Campbell, 2019b). Despite trending campaigns such as #FilterDrop (see Hallett, 2020), encouraging people to post images without any editing or filters, and strategies employed by social media platforms such as the moderation of pro-eating-disorder hashtags and hiding 'like' counts (see Sharp and Gerrard, 2022), young people are keen to keep up with the increasingly high beauty standards in the age of hyper-comparison.

Beauty standards and the role of modification apps can impact behavioural norms and values in a corrosive way and portray a version of reality that is doubtfully real. Clear examples of this were seen in participant attempts to create narratives about their identities through images. Both Sophie and Olivia spent many hours capturing the perfect make-up and body transformation images and videos to upload onto their Instagram accounts. Similarly, as described earlier in this chapter, Jessica and Elle arranged to go to an 'Instagram-worthy' bar to take photos for their accounts, and they frequently referenced the *Love Island* girls with their 'perfect' figures and appearances. Through the use of body and face modifying apps to see what a possible cosmetically-enhanced version of themselves would look like, the participants were embedding themselves within the environment of hyper-comparison, an environment that has fragmented the social life and atomized users, transforming them from friends into individual competitors engaged in the display of cultural capital. As such, young people have become the everyday producer and consumer of unattainable ideals through processes of 'prosumption' (Beer and Burrows, 2010).

The rise of the social media influencer

The digital revolution has not only changed the way the world communicates, it has also altered the way people can earn money and has given rise to a new category of 'social media celebrity' (Hou, 2018). The democratic nature of social media spaces has transformed celebrity culture, where creating and maintaining a celebrity persona is now something 'ordinary' people who are not celebrities can do (Banet-Weiser, 2017). This is distinct from traditional celebrity fame, which is often earned through achievements within specific industries (for example, film, music, sports) (Brooks et al, 2021). Social media enables individuals to have direct lines to the wider public, facilitating micro-celebrity fame to be generated through the creation of carefully curated online content, engaging with their audiences and self-branding (Khamis et al, 2017). Both Olivia and Sophie described themselves as 'social media influencers'.

Participating in the influencer industry became an enticing pathway for Sophie to gain income and a sense of security with her finances, and it enabled her to acquire 'celebrity capital' (Brooks et al, 2021) that would have been impossible to achieve in her full-time job. Sophie's route into social media influencing began during her early twenties when she documented her 'weight-loss journey' on Instagram in order to hold herself accountable and track her own progress. At the same time, she had a 'real' job as a self-employed eyelash technician, but 'job opportunities were few and far between' (Sophie). However, following an influx of 'followers', her increasing popularity on social media turned into a means to earn some additional money.

Through Sophie's industrious commitment to Instagram and subsequent YouTube channel, she quickly earned herself a prominent position as an influencer and began influencing consumer trends among her followers through the creation of content that featured her diet and exercise regimes, beauty tutorials, shopping hauls and 'day in the life' videos. This position involved enticing her social media followers into purchasing products, often in exchange for a range of economic benefits (for example, endorsement deals) and social rewards (for example, more followers, invitations to exclusive events) that would have been impossible to achieve otherwise. Despite Sophie's full-time job, she described herself in the 'Work' section of her Facebook page and 'Bio' of her Instagram account as being a 'social media influencer' and 'public figure'. With over 150,000 followers, her position as a fitness, dietary, beauty and fashion expert were validated by recognition and formalization on social media, rather than by professional expertise and training. Against the backdrop of heightened economic precarity and social upheaval, social media influencing can become a more viable career path for young people like Sophie.

Olivia was at an earlier stage in her social media career, and although she had a moderately large Instagram following of 60,000 followers, it was not substantial enough for companies to work with her. Social media influencers with large audiences are usually contacted by companies to promote their products in exchange for monetary gains or free products and services (Hund, 2023). Having previously worked in an industry where her income wholly depended on her appearance, Olivia understood the importance of looking good:

> I think I look good. I spend a lot of money on how I look, so I don't think it's too big headed to say that. I'm always in designer gear, work out five times a week, and take care of my appearance. It's like modelling work, you have to look good in this industry. People don't want to be influenced by someone who doesn't look like they have their shit together … to be someone worthwhile on social media, you need to look good. And do fun things.

Olivia's comment indexes the importance of physical appearance within a hyper-comparative and competitive individualistic environment. Although spending more time creating social media content led her to have a less stable source of income, the sense of cultural relevance and recognition that she was doing something worthwhile with her life was a driving motivation. Throughout the fieldwork, Olivia's following slowly increased and she began to promote products for various skincare and make-up brands in exchange for a low wage. Duffy (2016) calls this 'aspirational labour', where people work for low – or no – pay to reap the social and economic rewards further down the road.

The influencer phenomenon is both a symptom of, and response to, the economic instability following the global financial crisis and the broader changes in social institutions described in Chapter 2. The contemporary landscape of destabilized employment and the concomitant rise of insecure, zero-hour contracts has caused many young people to aspire to the role of 'influencing' on social media (Duffy, 2017). In the same way that young males aspire to make a living through streaming themselves playing video games via YouTube and Twitch, young females are aspiring to use social media as a form of paid labour. This is not to say that men do not engage in social media influencing in the same way. However, fashion, beauty and lifestyle blogging seem to be largely populated by young women (Duffy, 2016) and gaming cultures and communities appear to be more male-dominated (Duffy and Hund, 2019). Whether gaming or influencing, those with careers on social media are subject to a different set of performance metrics as they are driven by the number of likes, followers, views and comments they receive.

Changing expectations of 'normal'

With increasingly more 'peers' against whom young people can judge their bodies, appearances and levels of material success, virtual culture provided the participants with heightened opportunities for hyper-comparison. The comparisons with others ranged from examining the clothes they were wearing, to how they (cosmetically and digitally) changed their faces, to how they received affirmation on their looks and measured their own varying levels of success. These comparisons had taken hold of the participants' engagement with social media, and the deceptively simple act of posting a photo was instead a labour-intensive task to ensure the right image was used and properly edited and that a standout caption was included prior to the post being uploaded. For example, Sophie spent many hours each day constructing the 'perfect' visual of herself to upload:

> It's not as simple as taking a quick snap and uploading it. I have to find a good location, take hundreds of photos, select the best one and edit it to make sure the lighting etc is perfect. I use an app on my phone to hide my spots, whiten my teeth and things like that. It's simple to use. I don't think people realize how much effort goes into a post. I have to make it look as natural as possible too. When editing photos, you don't want people to know they've been heavily edited. Even though

> we all do it, you still have to try and make it look like you don't. It's got to be realistic.

Carefully constructing the self to appear authentic was fundamental for economic and social capital. To get by in the influencer industry, social media users like Sophie are expected to carefully navigate between being authentic and idealized and being 'real' but not 'too real' (Hund, 2023: 74). As her position requires her to present herself and her lifestyle in a particular and appropriate way to help secure future work and more followers, it was perhaps expected that the photo aesthetic was crucial for Sophie. However, the blurring boundaries between what is 'real' and what is presented for entertainment is shifting expectations for society at large (Tiggemann and Anderberg, 2019). This meant that casual social media users also felt the pressure to present visually pleasing photos. As Grace shared:

> I wouldn't just upload anything to my Instagram. It has to be a good photo with a nice background and good lighting; otherwise, there's no point in uploading it. You should only put the best of the best photos up. And a good caption. I spend a lot of time trying different filters, editing tools and writing different caption ideas. Sometimes it would take a day or two for me to post the photo.

This example illustrates how the pressure to construct a 'perfect' image on social media is not limited to influencers, but it was also experienced by many regular social media users. Filters were a popular way to adjust the face and body to look better and keep up with the unrealistic beauty standards. With just one swipe on Instagram stories, users were able to apply various filters over their selfies, with many using the 'Paris' filter to brighten the face and remove pores, blemishes and any sign of wrinkles. The participants relied heavily on the post-production process, rather than the initial capture process itself, but the use of camera angles and lighting tools (for example, ring lights) to manipulate images, minimize wrinkles, hide blemishes and appear slimmer was still a common practice when capturing images. As 'prosumers' their engagement with appearance as a form of self-expression is also actively shaping and (re) producing beauty ideals. As such, technologically mediated images – of the self, of friends, of everyone – are becoming ever more idealized, unrealistic and out of reach. The notion of not using filters or editing tools on their photos prior to uploading to social media was deeply undesirable for the participants. As such, there is a continual reinforcing of what is considered 'normal' in which the physical and virtual self is in a continual search for enhancement and perfection (MacCallum and Widdows, 2018).

The desire to have an active presence online and create the 'perfect image' of the self within virtual and physical spaces was further intensified with the ongoing rise of reality TV. Programmes such as *Love Island* have served to push the boundaries of participatory culture through the exploitation of new forms of digital media. To this end, there has been the rise of an entire media ecosystem surrounding reality TV in which audiences not only watch such programmes but can simultaneously discuss the shows online through social media sites; follow the lives of the reality stars through their respective social media pages; download games enabling them to virtually experience the reality programmes; and 'shop the look' directly through the programmes' official app or secondary sources. In the case of *Love Island*, there have also been commercial partnerships with fast fashion and beauty companies such as Missguided, I Saw It First, Superdrug and Rimmel, where consumers like Carys were able to buy the same outfit and beauty products seen on the show:

> I love that they have that app now. I've bought a couple of the outfits I've seen the [*Love Island*] girls wearing on the show. It's nice to see someone in the outfit before you buy it, rather than just a photo on the website. It's a clever tactic really, especially as everyone wants to look like them.

Alongside this, adverts for breast enhancement surgery shown during *Love Island*'s advertisement breaks in 2018 (see Rawlinson, 2018) went beyond presenting the lifestyles of women who had breast augmentations in a positive light to imply that women needed cosmetic surgery to be truly happy with their bodies and enjoy an aspirational lifestyle. Such portrayals of an enhanced body and lifestyle are increasing the desire for a minimum standard of beauty and intimately shaping the cultural dissatisfaction with body image through feelings of shame, inadequacy and failure to meet the requirements to be 'good enough' (Widdows, 2018). These examples demonstrate how unrealistic expectations are clearly impacting young people's sense of objective reality, which can ultimately lead to individuals undertaking harmful beauty practices to achieve the desired look.

Audiences are continually inundated with unrealistic expectations of beauty and carefully curated versions of others. TV shows routinely feature the shame and suffering of the 'non-attractive', with reality TV itself inviting viewers into the apparently successful lives of the shows' subjects, and often focusing on life-changing cosmetic surgeries and enhancement journeys. At the same time, social media users post 'get ready with me' and makeover tutorial videos on a range of channels and are constantly projecting a highlight reel of their lives that makes it impossible for others not to compare themselves to (Freitas, 2017). It is unsurprising that it has become second nature for individuals to agonize over their appearance and the perception of missing vital milestones in life when comparing their realities to the representations of life they are experiencing through media. This was particularly true for the participants, who often compared the behind-the-scenes of their lives with the highlight reels of other people's lives.

Additionally, public broadcasting of celebrity daily life has made celebrities a lot more relatable to the 'ordinary' person, and as more 'ordinary' people are attempting to become micro-celebrities, celebrities are appearing more normal and their status achievable. For example, celebrity lives can now be framed in the same newsfeed as friends, allowing individuals to seamlessly scroll from a friend's new Mulberry handbag to Kourtney Kardashian's morning chai, making the lives of the rich seem less far-fetched and more relatable than ever. The ease of following, observing and monitoring the positive outcomes and affirmations those in the public eye receive for their appearance have inevitably pushed consumers like Sophie, Grace and Carys towards emulating such celebrity presentations through developing their virtual and physical selves, according to the content they are consuming. In addition to the presentation of idealized body images, the internet and social media platforms are now awash with images of facial and bodily cosmetic enhancements and transformations. During my time in the field, I encountered images of certain procedures, treatments and products trending on Instagram, Facebook and X (formerly Twitter) using hashtags such as '#LoveIslandLips', '#KylieJennerPackage' and '#MarbellaLips'. The pervasiveness and accessibility of these images, alongside advertising and celebrity and influencer endorsements through the internet, have encouraged changing attitudes and the growth of the industry. Given the rising demands of beauty and appearance, it is no surprise that the beauty, fitness and health industries have boomed in recent decades. The participants were constantly on the lookout for new commodities and experiences that 'promised' to provide pleasure, satisfaction and fulfilment, and helped them pursue the 'ideal perfection' of consumer capitalism's identity-orientated culture. Within a hyper-comparative and competitively individualistic environment, beauty products and procedures promised them exactly that: the reaffirmation of their individuality, the elicitation of envy within others, the avoidance of cultural obsolescence and the enhancing of their appearance facilitating their position within exclusive communities (discussed in Chapter 7).

The consumption of beauty products is ideologically and practically normalized and the requirements for sustaining the minimum standards of beauty for the participants was demanding. As demonstrated in Chapter 5, many individuals were accustomed to working in (legitimate and illegitimate) jobs that required them to conform to certain beauty standards and maintain attractive and well-groomed appearances. With the rise of increasingly unrealistic beauty ideals, consumers were willing to endure potentially risky and extreme practices, including the use of 'under the counter' products,

DIY Botox and dermal fillers and self-prescribed weight-loss drugs, to meet such standards. Additionally, the acquisition of such products and procedures typically involved a combination of readily available consumer credit through overdrafts, credit cards, loans, further indebting the participants as they spent beyond their means in their quest to aesthetically enhance and display their face and body in both physical and virtual spaces. These behaviours mirror and align with Widdows's (2018: 101) notion that 'no matter what your resources, the message is you can, and the implication is you should, engage in the daily routine of beauty'.

Those involved in my research were all either living in debt or stuck in an endless cycle of being in debt within days of being paid; they prioritized their beauty and fitness regimes and social lives above all else. During a conversation on payday, Elle and Jessica discussed how their desire to indulge in consumer and leisure markets would leave them struggling with money each month:

Elle: Did you get paid today?

Jessica: Yeah, thank God. It's been such a long month, hasn't it? … I'm already back in my overdraft though.

Elle: That's usually me in the second week of getting paid, not the first! I've got about £300 to spend this month, but I'm getting my hair, nails and eyebrows done next week. And we still have to fork out for [the Botox party and night-out] tomorrow. And I need to get a new dress for it. I'll probably be in the same situation as you after that.

Jessica: I've already spent £250 this morning. I got a bit over excited and did some online shopping. I still need to pay my credit card off too … I'll come with you next week to get my nails and eyebrows done though. I'll whack it on my [credit] card and hopefully get some good tips [at work] this month.

While Jessica worked a low-paid job at a local café, Elle was an assistant buyer for a fashion company in the city and she was the only participant to have a full-time, 9 to 5 job. This, however, did not leave Elle in a better financial situation than other participants, and she frequently dipped into her overdraft each month. As consumers are constantly working to pay off debt, they are also increasingly considering the removal of consumer debt as an important life goal (Lazzarato, 2015). For the majority of them, they were working in jobs they hated in order to pay back what they owed. This became a psychological burden for many, as the allure of consumption faded and left behind a sense of hollowness and, of course, an uncomfortable amount of debt which relied upon their willingness to continue living 'deferred lives' (Davis and Cartwright, 2019).

The pressure to enhance and maintain appearance and identity resulted in unsustainable bouts of spending which left consumers, like Elle and Jessica, struggling for money until the next payday (Dittmar, 2008). Further, Lauren also embraced the philosophy of earning money and spending it straight away, which is indicative of the centralization of consumption in everyday life (see Bauman, 2007). Lauren regularly went to social events, had Botox and dermal filler treatments and frequented beauty salons at least once a week. She had professionally whitened teeth and would only wear clothes with visible designer logos. Given the financial demands of her beauty commitments and social and leisure activities, alongside selling illicit goods Lauren took out a credit card to help finance the consumer lifestyle she desired:

> I like to spend money on my appearance. It makes me happy, and if I couldn't afford to get filler or my nails done, I wouldn't feel like myself anymore. I'm not one of those people to give up on themselves because times are tough. When I see people like that, I think if you can't afford what you want, consider a side hustle to earn extra money. Don't just be a nobody … People my age are trying to save for a mortgage, but I don't see the point. If I saved what I earned, then I could, but that's not top of my priorities right now. I'd love my own place, but for now, I'm happy renting, living my life, and working on becoming the best version of myself.

Spending beyond her means on her appearance and a leisure lifestyle is symptomatic of the widespread 'culture of indebtedness' (Horsley, 2015) which categorizes life in the twenty-first century (Lazzarato, 2015). This normalization of indebtedness can be seen through the ways in which such messages are communicated in advertising. For instance, Master Card's 'Start something priceless' TV advert aims to encourage individuals to impulsively spend on credit to feed self-indulgence, while prompting the strategy of 'do it now, think later'. In the UK, living on debt and in credit has 'become part of the national curriculum, designed, endorsed and subsidised by the government' (Bauman, 2007: 79). For example, students attending university in England are expected to take out student loans to the value of £9,000 per year for the duration of their degree. In recent years, such loans have become increasingly insufficient at covering the rising living costs of students who are having to take up additional work or utilize other forms of finance to supplement such costs (Davis and Cartwright, 2019; de Ferrer, 2023). Not only are people increasingly prepared to go into debt to finance their education, but many are now turning to debt to finance their consumption practices of luxury branded products, younger-looking faces, bigger breasts and flatter stomachs in an attempt to keep up with the rising beauty demands. This has certainly prompted growing mental health issues among young people including depression and anxiety (Wickham et al, 2020).

'If you didn't post it on Instagram, did it really happen?': will to representation

The abundance of social media platforms allows users into the carefully curated lives of others as constant streams of photographs and videos flaunting consumer goods, lifestyles and experiences are uploaded. From holidays in the Maldives and extravagant homes, to eating and drinking at expensive restaurants and bars and buying the latest consumer items, the participants aspired to emulate the envy-eliciting visuals, videos and TV shows they were consuming. In particular, the Clique spoke of the YouTube phenomena of 'clothes hauls', where a previous contestant from *Love Island* had 1.1 million views for announcing her new collaboration with a fashion brand and showed off the latest items she had purchased. However, consistent observation of celebrities and influencers can cause a widening of the gap between hope and reality (Irwin-Rogers, 2019) as individuals constantly chase an exponentially increasing level of material wealth. This constant exposure to the perceived successful lives of others is trapping younger people in an endless cycle of hyper-comparison in which they repeatedly judge themselves against social media imagery and their peers from around the world. The participants were not shy in flaunting and discussing their latest (counterfeit and non-counterfeit) purchases online and in-person. To give a few examples: Brandon's calculated tour of his house to show off his latest consumer purchases; Jessica showing off her branded make-up in the middle of a bar; Olivia's 'My Cosmetic Journey' YouTube video that informed her social media followers of her procedures; and Sophie documenting her weight-loss journey on social media.

Online spaces provided the participants with an opportunity for presenting the self, and the hyper-comparison that permeates contemporary society appeared to be a catalyst behind young people's compulsion to share every achievement, goal and activity, to display economic success, to showcase highly luxurious consumer lifestyles and share consumption practices. The participants conceded that 'If you didn't post it on Instagram, did it really happen?' (Carys), where the act of sharing on social media was just as important as the actual consumption practices. This is part of the contemporary 'will to represent', where consumers presented idealized images of the self and carefully constructed online personas through the careful curation of content with the 'desire for social recognition through self-representation' (Yar, 2012: 252). From new jobs, acquiring the latest trainers, booking expensive holidays and having a new cosmetic injection, to completing a run, getting tickets to a festival and sharing their location from a quirky bar, it was perhaps no surprise that there was a constant urge for the participants to document everything on social media.

Virtual communicative spaces rewarded them with instant gratification and an abundance of external validation; this was usually in the form of likes, a thumbs-up emoji or social connections in the form of an increase in followers or friend requests. Such features are designed to activate the brain's reward system and keep people invested in the platforms (Meshi et al, 2015). The act of being validated by others taps into young people's neurochemistry, and as the participants demonstrated, when an individual receives an influx of positive attention on social media it leaves them feeling like they are, at least for the time being, 'popular', 'worthy' and accomplished. The positive feelings, however, are fleeting and, as they fade, the same insecurities begin to resurface as the individual hyper-compares themselves to others who have more likes, more comments or more friends, which, of course, elicits envy and fuels desire.

Olivia and Sophie both devoted significant time and attention to their social media personas due to their positions as social media influencers. They understood the importance of a physical aesthetic that lived up to the demands of online visual culture through the display of acceptable brands, luxurious holidays, enhanced faces and bodies, and attending social events. Sophie was frequently 'gifted' beauty, fitness and food products by companies to promote and advertise to her followers and she had secured herself a paid partnership with a fitness brand to showcase its gym wear. She had always been upfront with her followers about brand deals and sponsorships and would not endorse products she did not believe in or enjoy. Endeavouring to make herself as 'real' and 'transparent' with her followers as possible, Sophie would also do (unpaid) live streams on Instagram to answer questions and share the physical changes she had made to her body:

> I try and keep it as real as possible. I don't think there is any shame in having work done so young. I find it weird when people say they haven't had work done when they clearly have. I always share with my followers how much more confident I feel now I've lost weight, had work done and gotten regular sunbeds. I get some messages saying, 'You're setting a bad example for young people', but I think not talking about it is just blindsiding people, which is far worse.

Sophie was 18 when she first had Botox, and 20 when she had dermal filler. Her openness regarding facial enhancements was not uncommon on social media. However, as Hund (2023: 141) argues, 'being real' on social media 'can only provide an illusion of reality', which can cause significant harm to individuals and society more generally. Sophie, like other fitness and beauty influencers, provide their audiences either implicitly or explicitly with the opportunity to compare and potentially adapt their own beauty practices in line with the content they are consuming. Such incessant engagement and consumption contribute to the hyper-comparison and harm that permeates everyday life.

Olivia also prided herself on 'keeping it real' online and often created content surrounding her experiences with her breast augmentation, rhinoplasty, Botox and dermal fillers. Although Olivia did not disclose the illicit nature of her cosmetic enhancement procedures, she created a YouTube video called 'My Cosmetic Journey' where she sat and talked to the camera for around an hour about her procedures and experiences. Such boundaries to the information that is revealed demonstrates 'the double bind in which many influencers find themselves, navigating the impetus to be real, but not so real that they alienate followers' (Hund, 2023: 57). Further, this need to address and reveal every experience, purchase and achievement through social media illustrates how young people are 'intimately entwined' with their 'will to representation' and desire to be seen by others (Yar, 2012: 254). Photos would be staged and heavily edited, products would be promoted, and they worked diligently to build and maintain relationships with their audiences. This form of identity construction through the acquisition, consumption and display of material and symbolic goods was not only shared by those who 'lived' on social media. Even those uploading to Instagram occasionally, for fun, elucidated the importance of posting the 'perfect' image which captured and represented their identity. As such, young people like Sophie and Olivia attempted to reproduce who they are through the visual publication of an idealized self-image (Smith and Raymen, 2018).

This 'doing it for the 'gram' (Jessica) mentality extended beyond social media influencers (Hund, 2023), where the participants were partaking in Instagrammable experiences to gain validation from their peers. The heightened pressure and desire of feeling worthy, of having something to broadcast to others, and to show their friends and peers their success was rife within the participants, who were anxious about needing to find the next thing to share with their audience. This included working towards announcement-worthy goals and judging personal success (and other people's success) through both the quantity and quality of those announcements in terms of the engagement such posts received through likes and comments. On one such occasion when I went shopping with Lauren, she was looking for a new dress that she would wear to take a selfie for her Instagram account. The purpose behind this was for her to announce her achievement of hitting a one stone weight-loss goal. But once this goal had been reached, others took its place. She spoke of wanting to hit other fitness goals including recording and uploading a video of herself squatting 50 kg at the gym, but for this to happen she needed a new gym outfit that she hoped would increase her chances of positive social media engagement. Therefore, the conditions present in late capitalism facilitate the proliferation of harmful behaviours underpinned by the quest for the acquisition of 'ideal perfection'. Thus, this contemporary 'will to represent' extends the dominance of ideals as young people's awareness of the economic and social rewards from selling, buying and using particular products, procedures and services increases.

Chapter summary

Given the increasingly large amount of time people spend in virtual spaces, there can be no doubt that such digital engagement and exposure is impacting young people's sense of objective reality (Hall, 2019). Whether constructing an image of the self to post, endlessly scrolling through social media newsfeeds, or commenting on and liking photos of others, the participants were constantly judging their bodies, appearances and levels of material success against visual images across global virtual culture (Irwin-Rogers, 2019). Through self-modification apps and technological filters, unrealistic and unattainable images of perfection and beauty have become a part of the fabric of lived reality (Widdows, 2018).

As the expectations of what is considered 'normal' rises, it is hardly surprising that many of these young people have distorted ideas and views on what is natural, unnatural, realistic and unrealistic. With so much pressure to have pixel-perfect skin, young people are injecting potentially harmful amounts of Botox and dermal fillers into the face to emulate their curated digital representation (Hall, 2019). Clearly, capitalism is not only discernible in moulding the harmful actions of people but also in shaping their subjective experiences.

7

Botox, Booze and 'Bonding'

Introduction

Following on from the investigation of how unrealistic ideals are impacting young people's sense of objective reality and the consequences and impact that hyper-comparison has on risky beauty consumption patterns, this chapter turns to how hyper-comparison among female friends takes place in real-life settings. Part of the work in this chapter revisits material from the Botox party discussed in Chapter 4. Here, this work further examines the informal nature of these parties and the interconnections between the supply and consumption of Botox. The first half of this section focuses on the Botox parties and how consuming beauty together was vital for this female friendship group known as the 'Clique'. The second half turns to the Clique's intense fashion and beauty regimes that took place before the 'big night out'.

The role of Botox parties

As demonstrated in previous chapters, beauty products and procedures were very much a tool for the late-capitalist consumer, fulfilling a range of everyday functions. These include the enhancement of the face; increasing the chance of securing a job or further work; and to regain a sense of control over their everyday lives. They are also fundamental in improving social standing and leisure experiences and for facilitating and maintaining friendships. Beauty products and procedures have always enabled group bonding and facilitated social interactions, particularly with strangers, by providing consumers and suppliers with a common ground (Black, 2004). Throughout my time in the field, it was rare to walk into a hair, beauty, nail or tanning salon and not see strangers talking to one another. Botox parties performed this social function for the Clique with the supply and use of (counterfeit) Botox and dermal fillers, alongside other beauty products and procedures, facilitating and providing that sense of belonging and community to its members.

Using both counterfeit and non-counterfeit beauty products was a way to enhance image and appearance together in attempts to conform to gender norms and beauty ideals through the conspicuous display of pecuniary strength and avoiding cultural obsolescence through inciting envy in others (Veblen, 2005).

Botox parties represent a discreet and distinctive mode of engagement with cosmetic enhancements, yet one that has received little attention in research. During my time in the field, it became increasingly evident that Botox parties were centred around consuming facial injectables, spending time with friends and consuming alcohol. The parties took place three to four times per year and, although the parties were the fundamental reason the Clique became friends, a lot of other activities emerged from this. The women from this group met up every Friday for a pamper night, and the next day was always followed by a night out. Indeed, Botox parties and female gatherings to 'get ready together' before nights out represented another space for hyper-comparison. Additionally, there would be other social events throughout the week including shopping trips, beauty appointments and weeknight drinks, but unlike the weekend these activities were not deemed compulsory by the group's standards. A shared commitment to fashion and beauty reinforced the group dynamic for these women; it functioned as a tool to create bonds and intimacy, allowing the formation of such a tight-knit friendship group.

Friday night at Reanne's: "it's a Botox party!"

> It was Friday evening, and the whole group arrived at Reanne's house for a Botox party. As Carys began setting up in the adjoining living room, where the procedures took place, the rest of us sat in the dining area, drinking Prosecco and discussing tomorrow's night out in the city. Having already attended one Botox party and several other social gatherings with the Clique, I felt relaxed and comfortable enough to join in the conversations. About 15 minutes after I arrived, Reanne went into the living room. She lay down on the sofa and I witnessed Carys put a needle into Reanne's lip. Minutes later, Elle and Olivia also moved into the living room area, while I remained at the dining table with Jessica and Elle. Without any probing, the conversation effortlessly switched from Jessica's dating life to the value of being a member of the Clique and attending Botox parties. (fieldnote)

Jessica: [Botox parties] are such a big event on our social calendar. A lot of people frown upon the idea of them, but we all know they are nothing like what you read in the news. And being able to do it together is just such a good bonding experience, especially as it's our little secret thing. Obviously, people know we have had work done [laughs], but not that we have these parties or how cheap we get it ... It's so nice to be part of our exclusive group where we all have the same interests. We are known for looking good, and I don't think that's vain to say. We spend so much time on [our appearances].

Elle: We all get a boost in confidence, have girly chats and drink Prosecco. It's just an escape from the real world. Every Friday we meet to have a girly pamper night, we have some drinks and that, but the Botox parties are just our favourite sort of nights ... Other people sometimes turn up on the other Friday nights, but not for Botox parties. That's just for us, the core members of the group. It makes you feel like you are part of something. And then every Saturday we get all dolled up together and head into town feeling so zen, refreshed and confident.

Jessica: The nights out are always so good! We are all on cloud nine. We aren't like other people ... [pause]. I don't mean this in a shallow way, but a lot of people let themselves go. Like, on nights out I look around and think, why would people let themselves look like that? I suppose we just aren't like that, so we don't understand it. That's why we all get on so well though. We have the same interests and values in terms of our appearance ... We have a distinctive style. Every time we go out, we see a couple of people wearing the same dress or something. It's never happened to any of us. It's like people don't have a mind for themselves. Not us though, we aren't clones. We are cool trendsetters. People always say how trendy we are.

What is important to observe from this discussion is not just the value and significance of beauty use, but how it contextualized their distinct identities in relation to others. Cosmetic enhancements, lifestyle drugs and cosmetic surgeries promise to make the subject stand out from the masses, reaffirm their individuality and enhance appearance and image, all of which 'promise' happiness and to aesthetically, emotionally and physically complete the subject (Bauman, 2001; Hall et al, 2008; Ayres, 2019). As such, this group of friends differentiated themselves from others through a long period of deep, immersive beauty use and fashion consumption which was essential to become an exclusive member of the Clique. They perceived themselves as distinct and unique, elevating themselves above the fashion victims they encountered on nights out. Additionally, they distinguished themselves from everyone outside of the Clique, disparaging the repetitive appearances and dress choices of others in the night-time economy (NTE), by describing them as 'clones' without a 'mind for themselves'.

This desire to distinguish themselves within the competitive NTE, and contemporary society more generally, led them to drastic measures in which they were injecting potentially harmful amounts of Botox and dermal fillers into their faces as they endeavoured to improve their appearance and image as part of the Clique. Yet, the potentially harmful nature of these substances is, of course, constantly disavowed. Observations in spaces of beauty and cosmetic enhancement use and supply revealed this intensified form of socio-symbolic competition, where 'friends are competitors in the circuits of consumption' (Smith and Raymen, 2018: 71). Botox, dermal fillers, make-up, fake tans and clothing choices within the NTE was about the conspicuous consumption of expensive products and brands that denote perfection, wealth and status. In particular, the Clique saw themselves as elite beauty consumers and better than other groups of friends and consumers of cosmetic enhancements, demonstrating how competitive individualism and hyper-comparison are driving consumer culture forward. They indicated that a key appeal of Botox parties was not only that they engendered a sense of belonging, which came with shared beauty consumption, but they also provided a more affordable and fun way of enhancing the face.

As mentioned, attending Botox parties, pamper nights and weekend outings in the NTE was compulsory. If someone missed an event without an excusable reason, a period of alienation would likely follow; this usually involved a short period of ostracizing the non-attendee. If they were repeatedly not actively involved in the shared consumption of beauty, they would be at risk of being socially withdrawn and excluded by the rest of the group. As Elle elucidated:

> It can be a financial strain. Every week we end up spending so much money, but it's something I have to do. If you don't make an effort with friends or your appearance, you end up being irrelevant. And no one wants that … There was another girl in our group, but she was always too busy and started attending less and less. We stopped inviting her because there's only so much effort you can put into someone who has an excuse for everything … I saw her in town the other day. She looked so different. She had properly let herself go.

The Clique often spoke of the 'other girl', someone who frequently failed to attend the gatherings and was, thus, no longer allowed to be part of their group. Despite, the financial strain of attending each event, it was deemed necessary to maintain membership, as Grace stressed:

> We arrange the date [of the Botox party] months in advance to ensure everyone can attend. They are always on Friday nights, and we meet every Friday anyway, but it's just in case someone has a wedding or a

> family member's birthday or something … It's hard to fund, I don't have a real income. I'm the youngest and the only one at university. I live at home, which saves a lot of money, but I have to spend roughly the same amount as the others. Not turning up because you can't afford it isn't an option. It really is a Clique. If you don't turn up one week, you feel left out the next week. If you miss a couple [of weeks], you probably won't get invited unless you make a lot of effort and have valid excuses.

The establishment and maintenance of close friendships are for most young people instrumental, fragile and synonymous with leisure activities such as shared beauty consumption and taking part in the NTE (Hall and Winlow, 2005; Smith, 2014; Nicholls, 2019). This 'close friendship' appeared fragile and, as these young women illustrated, without engaging in these activities there would be no friendship at all.

Not only was it vital to attend the social events, but the shared nature of beauty rituals was also essential for these women. At each party, for example, there was an imperative for everyone to undergo at least one procedure, with several procedures being performed in one night. When I first met these women, Jessica was the only member of the Clique who had not had Botox or dermal fillers. Although she had wanted lip filler for many years, her fear of needles and the potential dangers associated with being injected with counterfeit products by someone unqualified was incredibly unnerving for her. Jessica had been attending the Botox parties for over a year, providing her with many opportunities to observe others being injected. But although this intensified the pressure to be injected to 'fit in', such frequent exposure to injections only served to reinforce the fear that something could go wrong:

> I know the girls have always been fine with it, but you hear stories about botched Botox all the time. Even though I've seen that Carys is good at what she does, there is always that risk isn't there? Something is going to go wrong at some point. I know that she isn't exactly … [pause] qualified. I found it all quite worrying because it gets injected into your face. You can't hide it … I know today is the day I need to go through with it. I don't want to be left out and not get invited, and I want to get them done … Pass me the Prosecco [Jessica downs a full glass].

Thus Jessica revealed the juxtaposition of her genuine fear and the longstanding desire to be injected. Despite the trepidation that something could go wrong, at the first Botox party I attended, and after copious glasses of Prosecco, Jessica was coerced by her peers into getting dermal filler injected into her lips. She admitted that she would 'drink to numb the pain' of being injected and appeared to show no concern for the increased dangers associated with being injected and alcohol consumption. By the end of the fieldwork, Jessica had been injected by Carys with both dermal fillers and Botox in various areas of her face and considered herself to be a 'real' member of the Clique.

The next day: getting ready together

The day after each Botox party involved a 'big night out' in the city. Going out in the NTE was entwined with the cultural injunction to enjoy (Žižek, 2002) and 'has become a compulsory part of contemporary society' (Ayres, 2019: 141). However, the 'getting ready' part of the night was just as important for these young women as it offered a specific opportunity to strengthen social bonds through the collective performance of beauty rituals and the construction of feminine appearances (Bancroft et al, 2014; Nicholls, 2019). The process of getting ready took place across multiple days. Alongside the hyper-normalized use (Cook and Dwyer, 2017) of (counterfeit) injectables the night before the event, there was an ongoing process of beauty maintenance throughout the week. The day of the night out then involved the use of beauty products, selecting clothing, styling outfits and a fashion show. The whole night appeared to be based upon hyper-comparison, competition and seeking recognition and validation from one another. As such, the process of getting ready to enter the NTE is also geared towards the construction and presentation of the self, and there were consequences among the group for getting it 'wrong'.

> It was the day after the Botox party, and I arrived at Reanne's house to attend my first night out with the Clique. The rest of the women were already there, sitting in separate areas of the room surrounded by large make-up bags, tanning products and the largest selection of make-up brushes I had ever seen. Each person had an A4 mirror propped up in front of them. The music was blasting out at full volume and the excitement for the night out was palpable. Reanne poured everyone a glass of Prosecco from the bottle, and I was instructed to take my belongings into the spare room where she had put up a clothing rail for us to hang our outfits on. I hung up my dress and headed back to the living room, where I was handed a mirror and drink. I stepped over the make-up bags and sat on the table opposite Jessica. Her excitement for the night was evident – she was not usually this talkative. (fieldnote)

Enthused, Jessica said:

> This is so cool, isn't it? Are you excited? It's going to be so much fun. I love that we all get ready together. How many houses have you been to where you get your own mirror on arrival? Reanne is

the best host … We don't have to rush to get ready either, as long as you are ready for about 8ish. We pick our outfits at around 7 pm, and then usually head to the bar at around 9 pm. But we have to leave time to get photos before. So we like to be ready by 8 pm. [The bar] has a good happy hour deal on Saturdays, until around 11 pm. It gets quite busy there, but we have a table booked so we should be fine. And then we will head to the [nightclub] after. It's going to be so much fun …

Suddenly, Reanne darted into the room and turned the music down. Looking rather concerned she asked, 'Have you only got one outfit with you?' This was followed by Elle, who said, 'What?! We always bring at least three with us. We take turns trying our outfits on and everyone votes on which one is the best.' They all seemed disappointed. Olivia asked if I could go home and get some more outfits. The conversation veered between me going home to get other clothes and me staying. This highly dramatic reaction often happens when someone does not follow the group's rules. At times I did not know when they were being serious but, luckily for me, Reanne realized she had forgotten to tell me to bring more than one outfit. They laughed it off. Reanne turned the volume of the music back up and the party atmosphere resumed.

Two hours into getting ready, after observing several meltdowns, the group had finally finished applying their fake tan, make-up, eyelashes and styling their hair. Next up was the big vote on outfits. As we all squeezed on the sofa, Grace emerged from the spare room wearing outfit number one. She was wearing a petite black dress and pink heels. Straight away the group said no, and she went to try outfit number two. Outfit two did not receive approval from the group either, but outfit number three was a success. They all took turns, and each person had three to four different outfits, two pairs of shoes and a whole range of accessories. It was around 45 minutes later, and Grace, Carys, Reanne and Jessica had all got the seal of approval. Next up was Elle. She walked out in a floral bodycon dress, and before she even got halfway into the room, Reanne loudly shouted from the edge of the sofa: 'Blimey, Elle, it isn't summer yet. It's raining outside. Is that seriously an option?' As laughter began to emanate from around the room, Elle attempted to laugh it off. It was clear she did not find it funny. She quickly went to get changed and came back into the living room to show her second outfit, a red A-line dress, and her third outfit, a sparkly black cami dress. The group were quick to dismiss all her options, and the tension in the room was palpable. Reanne took it upon herself to get Elle a new outfit from her wardrobe, and the group approved right away. The group then told Elle to change the colour of her eyeshadow and take her hair out of the updo

> she had spent the last hour doing. Elle looked very uncomfortable but conformed. (fieldnote)

Later in the evening, Elle reflected on the utter sense of self-loathing and worthlessness she felt when she was mocked by the others:

> It can be hard sometimes. Although we're all such good friends, it sometimes feels like we are in constant competition to look the best. I genuinely thought my outfits looked good. We all want each other to look good and be the best versions of ourselves, but sometimes it feels too much. I can handle criticism, but not when I'm made to feel like a joke. It made me feel like shit. I didn't even want to go out anymore … Don't get me wrong though, I love being a part of the group but sometimes I think everyone takes it a bit too far. It's hard to get it right every single time. Trends change, and people's opinions change. It's like a guessing game.

Belonging to the Clique was, in reality, socially hollow. Instead of being based on the 'long-term mutuality, reciprocity and loyalty that were core properties of traditional friendships' (Hall and Winlow, 2005: 34), the relations between the group were fragile and relied on superficial sociability and shared consumer experiences. Ayres (2019: 145) makes the point well by noting that in contemporary society, 'everything serves an instrumental purpose and once that purpose is fulfilled the object, person or experience is discarded to make way for a new one'. This is not suggesting that friendships always remain meaningless, but rather that these young women were basing their friendships on attending and being injected at Botox parties, religiously attending the weekly pamper nights and going out in the NTE each week.

While investment in femininity can have a high value for some women within friendship groups, a performance of femininity that was perceived to be incorrect or excessive can be ridiculed and devalued by others (Nicholls, 2019). These forms of monitoring and judgement were evident across the participants, with many young women and men divulging the pressure they felt to look a certain way in visual culture and real life. What is important to observe from the previous narratives is the centrality of feedback. The shared experience of getting ready together provided the Clique with another space for hyper-comparison, validation and reassurance. The structure and process of the fashion show encompassed the same structure and process of virtual communicative spaces for hyper-comparison such as Instagram. The social media user would upload a photo of themselves to seek reassurance and validation from others. If they received enough likes and positive comments, they would feel worthy (Meshi et al, 2015). If they did not, they would begin to feel increasingly more insecure as they compared themselves to others who received the desired positive feedback and validation. Even though the practice of getting ready together presented another opportunity to bond through the collective performance of beauty rituals, and allowed the participants to receive the valued opinions of one another, as the earlier example shows, even when participating they could still be at risk of becoming a figure of mockery and humiliation. Elle's failure to bring an outfit that exuded coolness resulted in feelings of personal inadequacy, humiliation and failure. As Winlow and Hall (2009: 95) suggest, these women sought to 'embody and display the difficult skill of being an individual at the same time as being a conformist'. This group of friends played a crucial role in encouraging and (informally) policing each other, with beauty and fashion decisions constantly being challenged. This was also extended to consuming facial injectables, whereby Jessica was expected to provide a satisfactory reason for not undergoing the needle. These women were, therefore, hyper-conforming to what is now heavily commodified femininity.

The pressure to conform to the commodified gender norms and the central tenets of neoliberalism was reinforced within the specific communities that comprised my fieldwork. While women such as the Clique got together to use Botox to conform to beauty ideals, the fieldwork also exposed how men would also get together to use melanotan II (M2) products within the gym environment as part of improvement rituals that centred on attempts to attain the idealized male body through bodybuilding. For example, within fitness communities some of Brandon's customers used M2 tanning injections as a result of the stereotypical hyper-masculine bodybuilder image. Whether through natural or unnatural, illicit or legitimate methods, observations within EvolveGym revealed a general theme among men with a muscular physique: they were all tanned. Further, using cosmetic enhancements and beauty products contributed to recreate standards and ideals that many young people are attempting to conform to. For example, every female participant in the study had lip filler to achieve the full-looking lip trend in contemporary society. Therefore, in addition to helping people stand out, they were also seen to help the young people within this study 'fit in', particularly with certain exclusive groups such as the Clique or within fitness communities.

Chapter summary

This chapter has served to consider the role of beauty consumption for social bonding within the context of Botox parties. Beauty use and injecting practices were a means of conforming to the commodified gender norms and the central tenets of neoliberalism. This chapter has examined how six of the female participants used (counterfeit) beauty as a form of female bonding, while simultaneously policing and criticizing each other's looks and behaviours in the competitive and comparative drive to look good. Overall, this chapter illuminated a significantly under-researched area surrounding the environment of hyper-comparison, the impact it has upon beauty use and injecting practices, and positions harmful consumption practices as a means of hyper-conformity.

8

Conclusion

Introduction

The Harms of Beauty has offered an insight into the wider life-worlds of consumers and sellers, following them not only as they engage with licit and illicit beauty markets, but also through their attempts to navigate a society characterized by hyper-comparison, hyper-consumption and competitive individualism. Recognizing the importance of online commerce and the internet, the empirical evidence from observations and interviews within online spaces (for example, social media sites, Facebook, Instagram and YouTube) has provided an understanding of the relationship between digital technologies, criminological activity, harm and the beauty industry. The concluding chapter will tie together the book's empirical findings with the theoretical context of this study. In doing so, it will answer the fundamental questions of why these young people use and sell counterfeit and illicit beauty products, and how they engaged with these products, before offering some recommendations to address these problems.

Aims of the book

This book set out to address the significant gap in knowledge regarding the broad range of harms related to the licit, illicit and counterfeit beauty industry and the willingness of individuals to self-harm and inflict harm on others and the environment in the pursuit of self-interest and 'ideal' perfection. Using life testimonies of young people, including numerous observations, informal conversations and interviews, I have tried to offer an alternative understanding of young people's involvement in illicit markets. In forging strong theoretical connections between harmful actions and the wider economic, social and cultural forces, structures and processes, this book offers a vital contribution to the criminological literature on counterfeits, crime and harm. Drawing upon advances in critical criminology (including ultra-realism, zemiology and deviant leisure), it offers a detailed account of subjective motivations and desires to reveal why young people are willing to inflict harm on themselves and others. It moves beyond the standard legal definitions of crime, and challenges existing debates which ignore the deeper harms that underpin the use and supply of counterfeit and illicit beauty products and services. Using a combination of traditional and virtual ethnographic research, this book offers an alternative understanding to the paradigmatic criminological framework of the counterfeit beauty industry. In taking this approach, it moves away from any further attempts to pathologize and label groups as 'deviant' and problematic. Echoing existing literature on counterfeit fashion consumption (Large, 2019) and consumer culture (Hall et al, 2008), I have argued that the fundamental drive to consume and supply counterfeit beauty products and services is symptomatic of hyper-conformity to the cultural values of neoliberal consumer culture. For the participants, the relentless use and supply of these products and services were far from being a sign of deviant or transgressive behaviour. Rather, such use represents the dedication and commitment that these young people have to consumer capitalism.

This book offers an insight into one facet of the harmful beauty industry, highlighting the nature of counterfeit consumption and supply, and the interconnection between the various spheres of consumers and sellers, supply and demand, online and offline and work and leisure. The 24/7 functioning of capitalism has blurred the boundaries between the various spheres of public and private life, work and social life, and leisure and consumption. In this all-consuming culture of self-presentation, separations between the physical and the digital have collapsed. In the context of contemporary beauty practices and consumption within Western culture, conventional physical spaces and digitally-mediated spaces are enmeshed (Crewe, 2017), connecting individuals and consumer communities on-demand. Therefore, I have argued that the virtual world now plays a significant role in local trade, beauty practices and the construction and transmission of harmful cultural ideals. Building on consumer capitalism's 'promise', I have argued that hyper-comparison is at the heart of contemporary society catalyzing widespread harm as individuals compete to be better, or at least appear better, than each other in the physical and virtual world. As such, this research has focused on the role hyper-comparison plays within young people's beauty practices, their sense of objective reality, the formation of their identity and their willingness to engage in harmful acts.

A primary focus of this book was to provide an interrogation of consumer motivations for buying and using counterfeit and illicit beauty products and services, informed by the broader political economy of consumer capitalism and advances in critical criminological theory. I have sought to overcome the limitations of existing perspectives on counterfeiting which have consistently eschewed a broader understanding of harm, consumption and global capitalism. In moving beyond such accounts of crime, harm and deviance I have produced a grounded analysis within a critique of the current landscape of consumer capitalism and have offered an argument examining the potentiality for myriad individual and social harms to occur. In centralizing the pernicious interconnections between an increasingly unstable and fluid job market, a culture of hyper-competitive consumer capitalism and a widespread culture of hyper-consumption and hyper-comparison, I have added to the understanding of the hyper-connectedness of work and leisure, supply and demand, and the online and offline spheres of life which are all reshaping the contemporary beauty industry and driving an increased demand for beauty consumption and consumer lifestyles that proliferate harm.

The contemporary seller and consumer lifestyles

One of the key findings of this book has been that the motivations of beauty consumers must be understood within the context of the environment in which they occur. In such a view, the motivations for selling were no different from the motivations to consume, all of which have been heavily influenced by the realities of late capitalism. Moving away from the existing research that has centred on the supply and consumption of counterfeits in a way that seeks to pathologize and label groups as 'deviant', this book provides a new perspective to understanding the harmful nature of counterfeit beauty markets in late capitalism. It illustrates how capitalism was discernible not only in moulding the harmful actions of the young people in this study but also in shaping their subjective experiences.

The empirical data provided in Chapter 4 has given insight into the operationalizing of contemporary illicit selling practices and the functional economic purposes they serve. For the participants, their selling practices did not align with traditional explanatory frameworks for understanding the motivations for selling counterfeits which often dominate criminology's theoretical repertoire, notably those that focus on the marginalized impoverished subject or the organized criminal who is going to invest their proceeds in illegal activities. Instead, the motivations and drivers for selling illicit beauty products and services were grounded in a variety of factors: the supplementing of legitimate income; to continue engaging with a desired consumer lifestyle; to obtain the feel-good factor of 'helping' others; and to increase their popularity as a seller and maintain friendships. Blurred boundaries between the producer and consumer allowed the participants to flexibly move between the two positions in the pursuit of their consumer lifestyle. Therefore, their behaviour can be conceptualized as being entirely conformist to the values of neoliberalism.

Further, although there was a high level of awareness in participant accounts of the potential for risk associated with buying and selling counterfeits, the money and friendships derived from these actions were nevertheless identified as sufficient motivators for engaging in risky behaviour. The ways in which the participants navigated and negotiated harm were guided by their own assessments of the risks and often focused on the potential harms facing them through possessing and selling the product, rather than through considerations of the potential harms and risks consumers and buyers of these products faced. Sellers appeared to be committed to the fact that they did not set out to harm others, nor did they derive any satisfaction or pleasure from such outcomes. However, the wider economic cultures shaped their behaviours as they were able to distance themselves from their actions, adopting a stance of resigned cynicism about the nature of the labour markets. Their accounts were based on the idea that if they could earn the money or access the products legitimately, they would. This was especially the case for David, who moved from drug dealing to counterfeit selling. Despite his dissatisfaction with the situation, he continued to sell counterfeits, highlighting the limited ability to withdraw their involvement from the systems they recognized to be harmful (Winlow and Hall, 2016). Participant perceptions of the broader economic landscape, therefore, played a vital role in their choices to engage in harmful behaviours. Finally, this work further demonstrates and contributes to research that positions and examines the intertwinement of legal and illegal businesses and how legal business relationships can be transposed into illicit business relationships (Antonopoulos and Hall, 2016). Indeed, as has been argued throughout, in order to produce an expansive understanding of the potential harms present within beauty consumption and production, both the licit and illicit markets and practices need to be understood in tandem.

Of course, the allure of money and consumer items that can be obtained through illicit selling is not a new phenomenon. For decades people have been willing to risk inflicting various types of harm on others as they seek to acquire material objects that symbolize status and success. Aside from David, it was clear that participants elicit an exaggerated commitment to a 'coherent and comprehensive socio-symbolic order based on meanings and codes' (Smith and Raymen, 2018: 72). The pressure for young people to construct and maintain identities through their consumer lifestyles is contributing to increased indebtedness among young people in contemporary society (Horsley, 2015). As consumer demand continues to grow, more young people are financially investing in themselves, searching for more affordable, but riskier alternatives to expensive products and procedures (Chapter 5). At the same time, they often accrue debt through such practices of consumption in vain attempts to satisfy unsatisfiable desires (Hall, 2019). The availability of easily accessible credit was instrumental in the lives of these young people, enabling them to engage in their desired consumer lifestyle despite not possessing the necessary income to do so in a responsible and sustainable manner. Under the guise of consumer 'convenience' there have been two significant developments towards a cashless society. The first of these developments has been the ability to seamlessly make payments using contactless forms of payment, or through faster payment systems, in which the body becomes the site of authentication through face identification or fingerprint recognition. The second has been the meteoric rise of 'buy now pay later' credit schemes such as 'Klarna' that build upon more traditional methods of credit cards and store cards. Combined, these methods mean that shopping for beauty has become a 24-hour experience in which consumers can conveniently purchase beauty and undergo beauty treatments within the comfort of their home, even if they do not possess the money to do so.

Instrumental motivations

Like other markets, beauty markets proffer solutions to problems of their own making. Beauty products and procedures provide 'go to' solutions for a range of problems including the uncertainties and difficulties in participants' working and social lives as a consequence of the precarity and instability of economic and societal transformations across the twenty-first century (Chapter 5). For most of those interviewed, the consumption of beauty products and procedures fulfilled a range of everyday functions in response to the increasing demands they felt were being placed upon them, including the need to meet beauty standards through enhancing the visual appearance of the face; improving social standing and leisure experiences; facilitating and maintaining friendships; increasing the chance of securing a job or further work; and to regain a sense of control over their everyday lives at a time of scarcity, precariousness and marketization.

In a competitively individualistic society, distinguishing oneself from the masses is deemed necessary and, as has been argued throughout this book, the pursuit and securing of an aesthetically pleasing appearance is considered a vital way of achieving this and of improving one's life chances. This was not just based upon the idea that altering the physical appearance would provide consumers with more confidence, but also that the products would help them gain employment and further their careers. For some participants (for example, Grace and Liam), consuming these products was seen as an investment for their future careers, offering them an edge in the job market.

Both legitimate and illegitimate work required participants to maintain attractive and well-groomed appearances. However, this rested on the ability to financially afford beauty products and procedures, driving many of the participants towards lower-cost, higher-risk alternatives to products and procedures. Almost all of the participants experienced a form of financial difficulty as a result of their spending habits, with most taking out loans, overdrafts and credit cards to subsidize their purchases. As beauty consumerism is ideologically and practically normalized, young people are conforming to ever more demanding beauty ideals in the pursuit of perfection. Many of the comments from participants were particularly apposite in light of what Widdows (2018: 101) suggests: 'no matter what your resources, the message is you can, and the implication is you should, engage in the daily routine of beauty'. Most participants were either living in debt or stuck in a cycle where they were back in debt within days of being paid; they prioritized their beauty and fitness regimes and social lives above all else. As consumers constantly working to reduce debt, they were also considering the elimination of consumer debt as an increasingly important life goal (Lazzarato, 2015). For the majority of them, they were working in jobs they hated in order to pay back what they owed. This became a psychological burden for many, as the allure of consumption faded, leaving behind a sense of hollowness and, of course, an uncomfortable amount of debt.

Socially corrosive harms associated with the beauty industry were also evident throughout the study. Such harms are prevalent within cultures in which precariousness and cut-throat individualism accompany a disregard for communal welfare and an overriding focus upon the self as manifested through leisure pursuits. The use of illicit beauty products and cosmetic enhancements, and their psychological and physical harm, has therefore become normalized. In a hyper-individualized, competitive consumer environment filled with hyper-comparison, the contemporary subject experiences anxiety and insecurity over their appearance along with increased pressures to maximize their own wellness. Such feelings combine to often make individuals feel worse about themselves (Cederström and Spicer, 2015). Beauty products and procedures are usually consumed as fundamental components of commodified leisure activities that occur in both virtual and physical spaces. Whether at the gym, on a night out, searching for Instagram fame or work, everyday life now appears to depend on bodily capital, and participants used beauty, fitness, health and wellbeing products and services in the pursuit of perfection, seeing them as not only part of a regime but also as a key part of their individual and social identities. These products and services promise the enhancement of the face, mind and body, enabling individuals to actively reconstruct their identities and project their self-images to others, which is capable of improving all aspects of public and private life. Beauty consumerism played a significant role in understanding the individual desire for self-improvement and the readiness of some consumers to engage in a range of harmful behaviours to fulfil their desires, conform to beauty standards, be aesthetically pleasing, and optimize their performance in the job market and within life more generally.

Hyper-comparison

Another key finding has been the role that hyper-comparison plays within young people's lives (Chapters 6 and 7). Aiming to add theoretical nuance to the existing work of ultra-realism, the concept of hyper-comparison has been introduced, drawing on the existing work of desire and the 'promise' of capitalism (McGowan, 2016). Within a culture of hyper-comparison, the participants were more willing than ever to inflict self-harm, harm on others and their environments in the pursuit of 'ideal perfection'. There were many examples where these 'friends' would compare themselves to one another. The young women from the Botox parties, for example, constantly competed (in virtual and real spaces) for attention by consciously displaying their desirable cosmetically enhanced faces and bodies. A notable example of this can be seen in Chapter 7, when the 'Clique' female friendship group took turns judging one another's overall appearance, competing with one another like it was a competitive sport. Even when they uploaded a photo to Instagram they would compare the number of social media likes they each received. However, the Clique's commitment and attachment to beauty appeared to be a consequence of the hyper-comparison between them. Such hyper-comparison entangled them in the 'increasing pressure to compete and perform conspicuously well' (Hall, 2019: 179) in ways that denoted wealth and status. I contend that the pervasiveness of hyper-comparison in contemporary society is a key catalyst behind beauty use and its widespread harm, one that is further intensified within virtual spaces as detailed in Chapter 6.

The development of this form of hyper-comparison is inextricably connected with the cultural and technological advances of late capitalism which place narcissism, competitive individualism and profound insecurity at the centre of everyday existence. From engagements, pregnancies, house purchases, bodily transformations, consumer experiences and everyday mundanities such as vacuuming the house, online spaces are spaces of announcement that perpetuate a desire to share the milestones and minutiae of contemporary life. Within such environments individuals are forever trying to be better, or at least appear better, than others. These effects are crystallized in the experiences of young people, as their engagement with digital platforms, and their consumption of distorted and edited images, filters into their lives, demanding them to look and be better. Such was the case with the participants, whose distorted views on what was considered natural and unnatural, realistic and unrealistic, were all heavily mediated by their engagement with, and consumption of, social media (Chapter 6).

This hyper-comparison among consumer subjects exacerbates feelings of inadequacy, dissatisfaction and absence (Lacan, 2007), and as subjects find themselves repeatedly cheated of the 'promises' of consumption they turn to potentially more harmful products and experiences to avoid their cultural obsolescence and social oblivion. The empirical data provided in Chapters 6 and 7 has demonstrated how such hyper-comparison is located in the portrayal of beauty in both online visual culture and in physical reality, and such imagery translates into intense desires to engage in practices that are deeply harmful. For participants like the Clique, this took the form of injecting potentially harmful amounts of Botox and dermal fillers into the face to emulate their curated digital representation, thereby conforming to the commodified gender norms and central tenets of neoliberalism.

Recommendations for future research and conclusion

By my account, this is the first ethnographic study that has attempted to understand the connections between the counterfeit beauty industry and the landscape of late capitalism. The findings of the research carry significant implications for the future theorization of beauty, harm and crime and emphasize the importance of reconsidering the many foundational concepts that have traditionally underpinned our understanding of counterfeit products. The common notion to address sellers and consumers of counterfeits as 'deviant' is problematic, and the motivations and actions of those engaging in harmful beauty and selling practices must be recognized as immanent in late capitalism in which the subject comes into being. Although this book has aimed to make a unique and timely contribution to the current literature, more work is needed to understand the connections between crime, harm and the counterfeit beauty industry in late capitalism. Further research is thus needed that not only moves beyond approaches that attempt to put the responsibility onto the consumer but also goes on to consider the normative assumption of 'choice'. This is because the roots of behaviours of those engaging in harmful beauty and selling practices are so deeply ingrained in the current system and, consequently, are beyond the individual's choice and control.

Theoretical understanding of why people are willing to inflict harm on others in this book indicates that the late-capitalist environment plays a fundamental role in shaping young people's motivations and their objective sense of reality. This book's extension of ultra-realist analysis into the study of the counterfeit beauty market has facilitated the theorization of beauty and illicit markets, moving beyond individualistic accounts that centre merely on economic rationalization for selling and buying counterfeits. It is thus imperative that criminological research continues to build evidence that can be used to create an alternative narrative capable of challenging the prevailing hegemony of neoliberal capitalism that is the dominant ideology of our times. The roots of behaviours need to be interrogated, as the late-capitalist landscape continues to produce new motivations, opportunities, pressures and anxieties for young people which combine to proliferate harmful actions that are, fundamentally, unavoidable.

Finally, I have established how the hyper-connectedness of consumers, sellers, work, leisure, and online and offline worlds are central for understanding contemporary forms of harm. This is not only due to the material opportunities they provide but also because they profoundly alter human experience and subjectivity. In forging strong theoretical connections between harmful actions and broader economic, social and cultural forces, structures and processes, the research contributes empirically to the wider attempts to understand young people's willingness to sell and buy beauty counterfeits, and to inflict harm on themselves and others. By illuminating some of the harms associated with the beauty industry in contemporary society, the project and its findings have contributed to a broader venture that extends beyond the ultra-realist criminological project into the fields of economics, sociology, politics, culture and psychology as they attempt to advance understanding of contemporary harm and, ultimately, to suggest more positive ways of organizing society and approaches to minimizing harm. It is imperative that cross-disciplinary research is undertaken to not only document these behaviours, but also to interrogate their roots and advance understanding of the market in counterfeit beauty. It is hoped that the ideas presented within this book can contribute to this.

Notes

Chapter 1

1 For some examples, see IPCG (2022) and Shepard et al (2023).

2 For some examples, see Antonopoulos and Hall (2015); Hall and Antonopoulos (2016); Antonopoulos et al (2018); and Large (2019).

3 All location and participant names used in the book are pseudonyms.

4 The Botox parties involved a group of female friends (Carys, Reanne, Olivia, Elle, Jessica and Grace) spending time together, using (counterfeit) facial injectables, and consuming alcohol.

5 A 'social media influencer' is a user who has accumulated a relatively large following and established a reputation for themselves by depicting their personal lives and lifestyles on social media (Abidin, 2016).

Chapter 2

1 For some examples, see Smith (2014); Ayres (2019); Hall (2019); Mulrooney and van de Ven (2019); and Gibbs (2023).

2 For a detailed description of the shift from industrial capitalism to low-wage service and leisure-based economies, see Winlow and Hall (2006); Hall et al (2008); Lloyd (2013); and Smith (2014).

3 As of April 2024, the UK National Living Wage is £11.44 per hour for those aged 21 years and over. Young people aged between 18 and 20 are entitled to the National Minimum Wage of £8.60 per hour; those aged 16 to 17 are entitled to £6.40 per hour.

4 Similar ethnographic studies found that illegal supply tends to be viewed as a foundational occupation in locales where participants disregard distinctions between 'legal' and illegal', viewing money simply as a means to achieving a better standard of living (Hall et al, 2008; Hobbs, 2013; Ancrum and Treadwell, 2017; Tudor, 2019).

Chapter 3

1 Melanotan I and melanotan II are unlicensed products and are illegal to purchase in the UK.

2 For example, retailers such as M&S and John Lewis have launched physical beauty drop-off points where consumers can drop off their empty beauty product packaging to stores. Additionally, consumers can return these through online websites such as Look Fantastic.

Chapter 4

1 This involved a four-week plan, where the minutes spent on the sunbed gradually increased each week.

2 All Botox parties were attended by a group of six friends who were all part of this research: Carys (28), Reanne (28), Olivia (25), Elle (23), Jessica (22) and Grace (18).

[3] 'The Clique' is a term these women repeatedly used to describe themselves. The use of the term 'Clique' is of high significance as it hints at the value they placed on belonging to something so exclusive (this point is developed in Chapter 7).

[4] UK law currently allows anyone – whether they are a medical professional or hairdresser – to administer facial injectables.

Chapter 5

[1] The Botulinum Toxin and Cosmetic Fillers (Children) Act 2021 came into effect on 1 October 2021 making it illegal to administer Botox or filler injections for a cosmetic purpose to people under the age of 18 years old.

Chapter 6

[1] Drawing from Lacan and Žižek, jouissance is an excessive, intense pleasure-pain that goes beyond useful and measurable. It is an extra element of pleasure attached to the painful experience of repeatedly never reaching one's goal. It transforms something or someone into an object of our desire that we can never quite reach.

References

Abidin, C. (2016) '"Aren't these just young, rich women doing vain things online?" Influencer selfies as subversive frivolity', *Social Media and Society*, 2(2): 1–17.

Ancrum, C., and Treadwell, J. (2017) 'Beyond ghosts, gangs and good sorts: commercial cannabis cultivation and illicit enterprise in England's disadvantaged inner cities', *Crime, Media and Culture*, 13(1): 69–84.

Antonopoulos, G. (2007) 'Cigarette smugglers: a note on four "unusual suspects"', *Global Crime*, 8(4): 393–8.

Antonopoulos, G., and Hall, A. (2015) 'The financial management of the illicit tobacco trade in the United Kingdom', *British Journal of Criminology*, 56(4): 709–28.

Antonopoulos, G., and Hall, A. (2016) '"Gain with no pain": anabolic-androgenic steroids trafficking in the UK', *British Journal of Criminology*, 13(6): 696–713.

Antonopoulos, G., Hobbs, D., and Hornsby, R. (2011) 'A soundtrack to (illegal) entrepreneurship: pirated CD/DVD selling in a Greek provincial city', *British Journal of Criminology*, 51(5): 804–22.

Antonopoulos, G., Large, J., Shen, A., Crang, M., and Andrews, M. (2018) *Fake Goods, Real Money: The Counterfeiting Business and Its Financial Management*, Bristol: Policy Press.

Appadurai, A. (1986) *The Social Life of Things: Commodities in Cultural Perspective*, Cambridge: Cambridge University Press.

Axford, I., Hill, S., Bird, G., Singh, S., and Macintyre, K. (2023) *A Feasibility Study Investigating Action Limits for Certain Heavy Metal Impurities in Cosmetic Products*, Office for Product Safety and Standards, [online] 16 March 2023, Available from: https://www.gov.uk/government/publications/action-limits-for-heavy-metal-impurities-in-cosmetic-products [Accessed 7 April 2024].

Ayres, T. (2019) 'Substance use in the night-time economy: deviant leisure?', in T. Raymen and O. Smith (eds) *Deviant Leisure: Criminological Perspectives on Leisure and Harm*, London: Palgrave Macmillan, pp 135–60.

Ayres, T. (2020) 'Substances: the luxurious, the sublime and the harmful', in S. Hall, T. Kuldova and M. Horsley (eds) *Crime Harm and Consumerism*, London: Routledge, pp 108–22.

Bancroft, A., Zimpfer, M.J., Murray, O., and Karels, M. (2014) 'Working at pleasure in young women's alcohol consumption: a participatory visual ethnography', *Sociological Research Online*, 19(3): 65–78.

Banet-Weiser, S. (2017) '"I'm beautiful the way I am": empowerment, beauty and aesthetic labour', in A.S. Elias, R. Gill and C. Scharff (eds) *Aesthetic Labour: Rethinking Beauty Politics in Neoliberalism*, London: Palgrave Macmillan, pp 265–82.

Bardey, A.C., Turner, R., and Piccardi, P. (2022) 'Bargaining our emotions: exploring the lived experience of purchasing luxury fashion counterfeit', *Strategic Change*, 31(5): 505–14.

Baudrillard, J. (1983) *Simulations*, New York: Semiotext(e) Inc.

Baudrillard, J. (1996) *The System of Objects*, London: Verso.

Baudrillard, J. (1998) *The Consumer Society: Myths and Structures*, London: Sage Publications.

Bauman, Z. (1992) *Intimations of Postmodernity*, London: Routledge.

Bauman, Z. (1998) *Work, Consumerism and the New Poor*, Buckingham: Open University Press.

Bauman, Z. (2000) *Liquid Modernity*, Cambridge: Polity Press.

Bauman, Z. (2001) *The Individualized Society*, Cambridge: Polity Press.

Bauman, Z. (2005) *Liquid Life*, Cambridge: Polity Press.

Bauman, Z. (2007) *Consuming Life*, Cambridge: Polity Press.

Bauman, Z. (2009) *Does Ethics Have a Chance in a World of Consumers?*, Boston, MA: Harvard University Press.

Bauman, Z. (2011) *Culture in a Liquid Modern World*, Cambridge: Polity Press.

BBC (2015) 'Rat droppings, urine and arsenic found in fake beauty items', BBC, [online] 18 May 2015, Available from: http://www.bbc.co.uk/news/uk-england-london-32772132 [Accessed 7 April 2021].

Beer, D., and Burrows, R. (2010) 'Consumption, prosumption and participatory web cultures', *Journal of Consumer Culture*, 10(1): 3–12.

Bell, B.T., and Dittmar, H. (2011) 'Does media type matter? The role of identification in adolescent girls' media consumption and the impact of different thin-ideal media on body type', *Sex Roles*, 65: 478–90.

Berkowitz, D. (2017) *Botox Nation: Changing the Face of America,* New York: New York University Press.

Bermant, C. (1975) *London's East End: Point of Arrival*, London: Eyre Methuen.

Bhaskar, R. (1997) *A Realist Theory of Science*, London: Verso.

Bian, X., Wang, K.Y., Smith, A., and Yannopoulou, N. (2016) 'New psychological insights into unethical counterfeit consumption', *Journal of Business Research*, 69(10): 4249–58.

Black, P. (2004) *The Beauty Industry: Gender, Culture, Pleasure*, London: Routledge.

Brannen, J., and Nilsen, A. (2002) 'Young people's time perspectives: from youth to adulthood', *Sociology*, 36(3): 513–37.

Brennan, R., Wells, J., and Van Hout, M. (2014) 'An unhealthy glow? A review of melanotan use and associated clinical outcomes', *Performance Enhancement & Health*, 3(2): 78–92.

Brennan, R., Wells, J., and Van Hout, M. (2019) 'Beauty through the eye of a needle': an online study of the practices and beliefs of people who inject performance and image enhancing drugs (PIEDs)', in J. van de Ven, K. Mulrooney and J. McVeigh (eds) *Human Enhancement Drugs*, London: Routledge, Chapter 10, pp 128–42.

British Association of Aesthetic Plastic Surgeons (2023) *Cosmetic Surgery Boom*, BAAPS, [online] 28 March 2023, Available from: https://baaps.org.uk/about/news/1872/cosmetic_surgery_boom/ [Accessed 20 November 2023].

British Beauty Council (2024) *The Value of Beauty: The Economic Impact of the UK Personal Care Industry in 2023 and 2024*, [online] July 2024, Available from: https://britishbeautycouncil.com/value-of-beauty-report-third-edition/ [Accessed 30 August 2024].

British Skin Foundation (2023) *Toxic Chemicals and Beauty Products: What Should Be Avoided and Why?*, [online] August 2023, British Skin Foundation, Available from: https://www.britishskinfoundation.org.uk/toxic-chemicals-and-beauty-products-what-should-be-avoided-and-why [Accessed 8 April 2024].

Brooks, G., Drenten, J., and Piskorski, M.J. (2021) 'Influencer celebrification: how social media influencers acquire celebrity capital', *Journal of Advertising*, 50(5): 528–47.

Brown, P., and Hesketh, A. (2004) *The Mismanagement of Talent: Employability and Jobs in the Knowledge Economy*, Oxford: Oxford University Press.

Brown, S. (2006) 'The criminology of hybrids: rethinking crime and law in technosocial networks', *Theoretical Criminology*, 10(2): 223–44.

Byrne, A., and Milestone, K. (2023) '"He wouldn't be seen using it …" Men's use of male grooming products as a form of invisible consumption', *Journal of Consumer Culture*, 23(1): 146–67.

Campbell, D. (1989) *The Romantic Ethic and the Spirit of Modern Consumerism*, London: Blackwell.

Campbell, D. (2019a) 'Call for tattooists and body piercers to qualify in infection control', [online] 14 June 2019, *The Guardian*, Available from: https://www.theguardian.com/politics/2019/jun/14/call-for-tattooists-and-body-piercers-to-qualify-in-infection-control [Accessed 20 March 2024].

Campbell, D. (2019b) 'Depression in girls linked to higher user of social media', [online] 4 January 2019, *The Guardian*, Available from: https://www.theguardian.com/society/2019/jan/04/depression-in-girls-linked-to-higher-use-of-social-media [Accessed 8 April 2021].

Carr, M., and Kelan, E.K. (2023) 'Between consumption, accumulation and precarity: the psychic and affective practices of the female neoliberal spiritual subject', *Human Relations*, 76(2): 258–85.

Cashmore, E. (2023) *Celebrity and Culture* (3rd edn), Abingdon: Routledge.

Castells, M. (2001) *The Internet Galaxy: Reflections on the Internet, Business, and Society*, Oxford: Oxford University Press.

Castells, M. (2010) *The Rise of the Network Society*, Oxford: Wiley-Blackwell.

Cederström, C., and Fleming, P. (2012) *Dead Man Working*, Winchester, UK: Zero Books.

Cederström, C., and Spicer, A. (2015) *The Wellness Syndrome*, Cambridge: Polity Press.

Chaudhry, P., and Zimmerman, A. (2013) *Protecting Your Intellectual Property Rights: Understanding the Role of Management, Governments, Consumers and Pirates*, London: Springer.

Cook, P.D., and Dwyer, A. (2017) 'No longer raising eyebrows: the contexts and domestication of Botox as a mundane medical and cultural artefact', *Journal of Consumer Culture*, 17(3): 887–909.

Coomber, R., Pavlidis, A., Hanley Santos, G., Wilde, M., Schmidt, W., and Redshaw, C. (2015) 'The supply of steroids and other performance and image enhancing drugs (PIEDs) in one English city: fakes, counterfeits, supplier trust, common beliefs and access', *Performance Enhancement & Health*, 3(3–4): 135–44.

Copson, L. (2018) 'Beyond "criminology vs. zemiology": reconciling crime with social harm', in A. Boukli and J. Kotzé (eds) *Zemiology: Reconnecting Crime and Social Harm*, London: Palgrave Macmillan, pp 33–56.

Cranswick, I., Richardson, D.J., Littlewood, M.A., and Tod, D. (2020) '"Oh take some man-up pills": a life-history study of muscles, masculinity, and the threat of injury', *Performance Enhancement and Health*, 8(2–3): 1–11.

Crary, J. (2013) *24/7: Late Capitalism and the Ends of Sleep*, London: Verso.

Crewe, L. (2017) *The Geographies of Fashion: Consumption, Space and Value*, London: Bloomsbury.

Cummings, S.R., Ling, X., and Stone, K. (1997) 'Consequences of foot binding among older women in Beijing, China', *American Journal of Public Health*, 87(10): 1677–9.

Currie, E. (2005) *The Road to Whatever: Middle-Class Culture and the Crisis of Adolescence,* London: Macmillan.

Davey, E. (2016) 'Illegal skin lightening creams being sold in London', [online] 17 February 2016, BBC, Available from: http://www.bbc.co.uk/news/uk-england-london-35589645 [Accessed 10 August 2023].

David, A. (2015) *Fashion Victims: The Dangers of Dress, Past and Present*, London: Bloomsbury.

Davis, M., and Cartwright, L. (2019) 'Deferred lives': money, debt and the financialised futures of young temporary workers', in M. Featherstone (ed) *The Sociology of Debt*, Bristol, UK: Policy Press, pp 91–118.

de Ferrer, M. (2023) 'Student maintenance loans almost entirely used up by rent, report warns', [online] 26 October 2023, BBC, Available from: https://www.bbc.co.uk/news/education-67206767 [Accessed 28 March 2024].

Demant, J., Bakken, A., and Hall, A. (2020) 'Social media markets for prescription drugs: platforms as virtual mortars for drug types and dealers', *Drugs and Alcohol Today*, 20(1): 36–49.

Department for Work and Pensions (2023) 'Government urges jobseekers to consider careers in "booming" beauty industry', [online] 27 October 2023, GOV.UK, Available from: https://www.gov.uk/government/news/government-urges-jobseekers-to-consider-careers-in-booming-beauty-industry [Accessed 30 January 2024].

Di Nicola, A., Martini, E., and Baratto, G. (2015) *Fake Care: Developing Expertise against the Online Trade of Fake Medicines by Producing and Disseminating Knowledge, Counterstrategies and Tools across the EU,* 02, eCrime Research Reports, Trento: ICT Law and Criminology, Faculty of Law, University of Trento, Italy.

Diefenbach, S., and Christoforakos, L. (2017) 'The selfie paradox: nobody seems to like them yet everyone has reasons to take them. an exploration of psychological functions of selfies in self-presentation', *Frontiers in Psychology*, 8(7): 1–14.

Dittmar, H. (2008) 'Understanding the impact of consumer culture', in H. Dittmar (ed) *Consumer Culture, Identity and Well-being*, Hove: Psychology Press, pp 1–24.

Dittmar, H., and Halliwell, E. (2008) 'Think "ideal" and feel bad? Using self-discrepancies to understand negative media effect', in H. Dittmar (ed) *Consumer Culture, Identity and Well-being*, Hove: Psychology Press, pp 147–72.

Duffy, B. (2016) 'The romance of work: gender and aspirational labour in the digital culture industries', *International Journal of Cultural Studies*, 19(4): 441–57.

Duffy, B. (2017) *(Not) Getting Paid to Do What You Love: Gender, Social Media and Aspirational Work*, New Haven, CT: Yale University Press.

Duffy, B.E., and Chan, N.K. (2019) '"You never really know who's looking": imagined surveillance across social media platforms', *New Media & Society*, 21(1): 119–38.

Duffy, B., and Hund, E. (2019) 'Gendered visibility on social media: navigating Instagram's authenticity bind', *International Journal of Communication*, 13: 4983–5002.

Dunne, A., Freeman, O., and Sherlock, R. (2006) 'Over-conformists to gender norms: anabolic steroid consumption among adolescent males', *Gender and Consumer Behaviour*, 8: 328–40.

Ecowatch (2023) 'Landfill of unused fast fashion clothes has grown large enough to be seen from space', [online] 24 May 2023, Ecowatch, Available from: https://www.ecowatch.com/landfill-clothes-chile-desert-fast-fashion.html [Accessed 27 May 2024].

Edwards, S. (2024) 'Shein suppliers still work 75-hour weeks – report', [online], 12 May 2024, BBC, Available from: https://www.bbc.co.uk/news/articles/cg67w73nxqxo [Accessed 25 May 2024].

Elias, A.S., and Gill, R. (2017) 'Beauty surveillance: the digital self-monitoring cultures of neoliberalism', *European Journal of Cultural Studies*, 21(1): 59–77.

Elias, A.S., Gill, R., and Scharff, C. (2017) 'Aesthetic labour: beauty politics in neoliberalism', in A.S. Elias, R. Gill and C. Scharff (eds) *Aesthetic Labour: Rethinking Beauty Politics in Neoliberalism,* London: Palgrave Macmillan, pp 3–50.

Elliot, A. (2013) *Reinvention*, London: Routledge.

Ellis, A. (2016) *Men, Masculinities and Violence: An Ethnographic Study*, London: Routledge.

ElShamy, A., and Cox, N. (2024) 'Luxury perfumes linked to child labour, BBC finds', [online] 28 May 2024, BBC, Available from: https://www.bbc.co.uk/news/world-middle-east-68172560 [Accessed 28 May 2024].

Entwistle, J., and Wissinger, E. (2006) 'Keeping up appearances: aesthetic labour in the fashion modelling industry', *The Sociological Review*, 54(4): 774–94.

Euromonitor (2019) *Beauty Survey 2019: Key Insights*, [online] Euromonitor International, Available from: https://go.euromonitor.com/white-paper-bpc-2019-beauty_survey.html [Accessed 28 June 2020].

Europol (2013) *EU Serious and Organised Crime Threat Assessment,* The Hague: Europol.

Fagan, J., and Freeman, R. (1999) 'Crime and work', *Crime and Justice: A Review of Research*, 25: 225–90.

Featherstone, M. (2007) *Consumer Culture and Postmodernism* (2nd edn), London: Sage Publications.

Featherstone, M. (2010) 'Body image and affect in consumer culture', *Body & Society*, 16(1): 193–221.

Fedorak, S.A. (2017) *Anthropology Matters* (3rd edn), Toronto: University of Toronto Press.

Fenton, S., and Dermott, E. (2006) 'Fragmented careers? Winners and losers in young adult labour markets', *Work Employment and Society*, 20(2): 205–21.

Ferrell, J. (2004) 'Style matters: criminal identity and social control', in J. Ferell and C. Saunders (eds) *Cultural Criminology Unleashed*, Boston: Northeastern University Press, Chapter 8, pp 61–6.

Ferrell, J. (2006) *Empire of Scrounge: Inside the Urban Underground of Dumpster Diving, Trash Picking, and Street Scavenging*, New York: New York University Press.

Fink, B. (1995) *The Lacanian Subject: Between Language and Jouissance*, Princeton, NJ: Princeton University Press.

Fisher, M. (2009) *Capitalist Realism: Is There No Alternative?*, London: Zero Books.

Fox, N., Ward, K., and O'Rourke, A. (2005) 'Pro-anorexia, weight-loss drugs and the internet: an "anti-recovery" explanatory model of anorexia', *Sociology of Health & Illness*, 27(7): 944–71.

Freitas, D. (2017) *The Happiness Effect: How Social Media Is Driving a Generation to Appear Perfect at Any Cost*, Oxford: Oxford University Press.

Friedman, G. (2014) 'Workers without employers: shadow corporations and the rise of the gig economy', *Review of Keynesian Economics*, 2(2): 171–88.

Gibbs, N. (2023) *The Muscle Trade: The Use and Supply of Image and Performance Enhancing Drugs*, Bristol: Bristol University Press.

Gimlin, D.L. (2002) *Body Work: Beauty and Self-Image in American Culture*, London: University of California Press.

Girlguiding Charity (2020) 'Girls fear criticism for being themselves', [online] 27 August 2020, Girlguiding, Available from: https://www.girlguiding.org.uk/what-we-do/our-stories-and-news/news/girls--fear-criticism-for-being-themselves/ [Accessed 28 June 2020].

Global Wellness Institute (2023) *Global Wellness Economy Monitor 2023*, [Online] viewed 15 November 2023, Available from: https://globalwellnessinstitute.org/the-2023-global-wellness-economy-monitor/ [Accessed 15 January 2024].

Gosse, C. (2021) '"Not the real world": exploring experiences of online abuse, digital dualism, and ontological labor', in J. Bailey, A. Flynn and N. Henry (eds) *The Emerald International Handbook of Technology-Facilitated Violence and Abuse*, Bingley, UK: Emerald Publishing, pp 47–64.

Grogan, S. (2022) *Body Image: Understanding Body Dissatisfaction in Men, Women and Children* (4th edn), Abingdon: Routledge.

Hackman, R. (2015) '"Beach body ready" tube advert protests planned for Hyde Park', [Online] 27 June 2015, *The Guardian*, Available from: https://www.theguardian.com/us-news/2015/jun/27/beach-body-ready-america-weight-loss-ad-instagram [Accessed 22 May 2017].

Hall, A. (2019) 'Lifestyle drugs and late capitalism: a topography of harm', in T. Raymen and O. Smith (eds) *Deviant Leisure: Criminological Perspectives on Leisure and Harm*, London: Palgrave Macmillan, pp 161–86.

Hall, A., and Antonopoulos, G. (2015) 'License to pill: illegal entrepreneurs' tactics in the online trade of medicines', in P.C. van Duyne, A. Naljevic, G.A. Antonopoulos, J. Harvey and K. von Lampe (eds) *The Relativity of Wrongdoing: Corruption, Organised Crime, Fraud and Money Laundering in Perspective*, Nijmegen: Wolf Legal Publishers, pp 229–52.

Hall, A., and Antonopoulos, G. (2016) *Fake Meds Online: The Internet and Transnational Market in Illicit Pharmaceuticals*, London: Palgrave Macmillan.

Hall, A., and Antonopoulos, G. (2019) 'The (online) supply of illicit lifestyle medicines', in K. van de Ven, K.J.D. Mulrooney and J. McVeigh (eds) *Human Enhancement Drugs,* Abingdon: Routledge, Chapter 13, pp 173–87.

Hall, A., Koenraadt, R., and Antonopoulos, G. (2017) 'Illicit pharmaceutical networks in Europe: organising the illicit medicine market in the United Kingdom and the Netherlands', *Trends in Organised Crime*, 20 (3–4): 296–315.

Hall, S. (2012a) 'The solicitation of the trap: on transcendence and transcendental materialism in advanced consumer-capitalism', *Human Studies: Special Issue on Transcendence and Transgression*, 35(3): 365–81.

Hall, S. (2012b) *Theorizing Crime and Deviance: A New Perspective*, London: Sage Publications.

Hall, S., and Jefferson, T. (2006) *Resistance through Rituals: Youth Subcultures in Post-War Britain* (2nd edn), Abingdon: Routledge.

Hall, S., and Winlow, S. (2005) 'Anti-nirvana: crime, culture and instrumentalism in the age of insecurity', *Crime, Media, Culture,* 1(1): 31–48.

Hall, S., and Winlow, S. (2015) *Revitalizing Criminological Theory: Towards a New Ultra-Realism*, Abingdon: Routledge.

Hall, S., and Winlow, S. (2018) 'Ultra-realism', in W. Dekeseredy and M. Dragiewicz (eds) *Routledge Handbook of Critical Criminology*, Abingdon: Routledge, pp 43–56.

Hall, S., Winlow, S., and Ancrum, C. (2008) *Criminal Identities in Consumer Culture*, Cullompton, Devon: Willan.

Hallett, E. (2020) 'Instagram photo filters targeted by model's #FilterDrop Campaign', [online] 7 September 2020, BBC, Available from: https://www.bbc.co.uk/news/uk-england-bristol-53784938 [Accessed 22 May 2023].

Hardgrove, A., McDowell, L., and Rootham, E. (2015) 'Precarious lives, precarious labour: family support and young men's transitions to work in the UK', *Journal of Youth Studies,* 18(8): 1057–76.

Harvey, D. (2007) *A Brief History of Neoliberalism*, Oxford: Oxford University Press.

Hayward, K. (2004) *City Limits: Crime, Consumer Culture and the Urban Experience*, London: Glasshouse Press.

Hayward, K. (2012) 'Pantomime justice: a cultural criminological analysis of "life stage dissolution"', *Crime Media Culture*, 8(2): 213–29.

Hayward, K., and Hobbs, D. (2007) 'Beyond the binge in "booze Britain": market-led liminalization and the spectacle of binge drinking', *The British Journal of Sociology*, 58(3): 437–56.

Hayward, K., and Turner, T. (2019) '"Be more VIP": deviant leisure and hedonistic excess in Ibiza's "Disneyized" party spaces', in T. Raymen and O. Smith (eds) *Deviant Leisure: Criminological Perspectives on Leisure and Harm,* London: Palgrave Macmillan, pp 105–35.

Hebdige, D. (1979) *Subculture and the Meaning of Style,* London: Routledge.

Hilton, B., Choi, C.J., and Chen, S. (2004) 'The ethics of counterfeiting in the fashion industry: quality, credence and profit issues', *Journal of Business Ethics*, 55: 345–54.

Hine, C. (2015) *Ethnography for the Internet: Embedded, Embodied and Everyday*, London: Bloomsbury.

Hobbs, D. (1988) *Doing the Business: Entrepreneurship, Detectives and the Working Class in the East End of London*, Oxford: Oxford University Press.

Hobbs, D. (1995) *Bad Business: Professional Crime in Modern Britain*, Oxford: Oxford University Press.

Hobbs, D. (1998) 'Going down the glocal: the local context of organised crime', *The Howard Journal*, 37(4): 407–22.

Hobbs, D. (2012) '"It was never about the money": market society, organised crime and UK criminology', in S. Hall and S. Winlow (eds) *New Directions in Criminological Theory*, Abingdon: Routledge, Chapter 15, pp 257–75.

Hobbs, D. (2013) *Lush Life: Constructing Organised Crime in the UK*, Oxford: Oxford University Press.

Holla, S. (2015) 'Justifying aesthetic labor: how fashion models enact coherent selves', *Journal of Contemporary Ethnography*, 45(4): 1–27.

Holliday, R., Meredith, J., and Bell, D. (2019) *Beautyscapes: Mapping Cosmetic Surgery Tourism*, Manchester: Manchester University Press.

Home Office (2022) *Intellectual Property Counter-Infringement Strategy 2022 to 2027*, [online] 4 February 2022, GOV.UK, Available from: https://www.gov.uk/government/publications/ip-counter-infringement-strategy-2022-to-2027/intellectual-property-counter-infringement-strategy-2022-to-2027#fn:10 [Accessed 22 May 2023].

Honneth, A. (1996) *The Struggle for Recognition: The Moral Grammar of Social Conflicts*, Cambridge: Polity Press.

Hooker, L. 'Retail: last year saw a big jump in the number of shops closing', [online] 2 January 2023, BBC, Available from: https://www.bbc.co.uk/news/business-64138898 [Accessed 2 March 2023].

Hope, M. (2024) *The Impact of Brexit on London's Economy – 2023 Report*, [online] January 2024, Greater London Authority 2024, Available from: https://www.london.gov.uk/business-and-economy-publications/impact-brexit-londons-economy-2023-report [Accessed 29 May 2024].

Hornsby, R., and Hobbs, D. (2007) 'A zone of ambiguity: the political economy of cigarette bootlegging', *British Journal of Criminology*, 47: 551–71.

Horsley, M. (2015) *The Dark Side of Prosperity: Late Capitalism's Culture of Indebtedness*, London: Ashgate.

Hou, M. (2018) 'Social media celebrity and the institutionalization of YouTube', *Convergence*, 25(3): 534–53.

Hua, W. (2013) *Buying Beauty: Cosmetic Surgery in China*, Hong Kong: Hong Kong University Press.

Hughes, D. (2017) 'Social media pressure is linked to cosmetic procedure boom', [online] 22 June 2017, BBC, Available from: http://www.bbc.co.uk/news/health-40358138 [Accessed 7 June 2020].

Human Enhancement Drugs (2017a) 'Image enhancing drugs', [online] Human Enhancement Drugs, Available from: https://humanenhancementdrugs.com/drugprofiles/image-enhancing-drugs [Accessed 2 February 2023].

Human Enhancement Drugs (2017b) 'Weight-loss drugs', [online] Human Enhancement Drugs, Available from: https://humanenhancementdrugs.com/drugprofiles/weight-loss-drugs [Accessed 2 February 2023].

Hund, E. (2023) *The Influencer Industry: The Quest for Authenticity on Social Media,* Princeton, NJ: Princeton University Press.

Hunt, Y., Augustson, E., Rutten, L., Moser, R., and Yaroch, A. (2012) 'History and culture of tanning in the United States', in C. Heckman and S. Manne (eds) *Shedding Light on Indoor Tanning*, New York: Springer, pp 5–31.

Hvass, K.K. (2015) 'Business model innovation through second hand retailing: a fashion industry case', in M. Gardetti, E. Rahbek and G. Pedersen (eds) *New Business Models for Sustainable Fashion: A Special Theme Issue of the Journal of Corporate Citizenship*, London: Routledge, pp 11–32.

IPCG (Intellectual Property Crime Group) (2022) 'Trading Standards success', [online], UK Intellectual Property Office, Available from: https://www.gov.uk/government/publications/trading-standards-successes-2021-to-2022 [Accessed 22 September 2024].

IPO (Intellectual Property Office) (2024) '"Choose Safe not Fake" campaign targets beauty and hygiene counterfeits' [online], 28 February 2024, GOV.UK, Available from: https://www.gov.uk/government/news/choose-safe-not-fake-campaign-targets-beauty-and-hygiene-counterfeits [Accessed 20 May 2024].

Irvine, J. (2017) 'ITV News investigates: India's shameful child labour mining for beauty industry sparkle', [online] 21 February 2017, ITV, Available from: http://www.itv.com/news/2017-02-22/itv-news-investigates-indias-shameful-child-labour-mining-for-sparkling-mica/ [Accessed 20 June 2020].

Irwin-Rogers, K. (2019) 'Illicit drug markets, consumer capitalism and the rise of social media: a toxic trap for young people', *Critical Criminology*, 27: 591–610.

James, O. (2010) *Britain on the Couch: How Keeping Up with the Joneses Has Depressed Us Since 1950*, London: Vermillion.

Jeffreys, S. (2014) *Beauty and Misogyny: Harmful Cultural Practices in the West* (2nd edn), Abingdon: Routledge.

Jewkes, Y., and Sharp, K. (2003) 'Crime, deviance and the disembodied self: transcending the dangers of corporeality', in Y. Jewkes (ed) *Dot.cons: Criminal and Deviant Identities on the Internet,* Cullompton, Devon: Willan, Chapter 1, pp 1–14.

Jones, M. (2012) 'Cosmetic surgery and the fashionable face', *Fashion Theory,* 16(2): 193–209.

Juggesur, J., and Cohen, G. (2009) 'Is fashion promoting counterfeit brands?', *Journal of Brand Management,* 16(5/6): 383–94.

Jurgenson, N. (2012) 'When atoms meet bits: social media, the mobile web and augmented revolution', *Future Internet,* 4(1): 83–91.

Kalleberg, A.L., and Vallas, S.P. (2018) *Precarious Work: Causes, Characteristics, and Consequences*, Bingley, UK: Emerald Publishing.

Keane, H. (2005) 'Diagnosing the male steroid user: drug use, body image and distorted masculinity', *Health: An Interdisciplinary Journal for the Social Study of Health, Illness and Medicine,* 9(2): 189–208.

Kelly, J. (2016) *Sweat Equity: Inside the New Economy of Mind and Body*, Hoboken, NJ: Wiley.

Khamis, S., Ang, L., and Welling, R. (2017) 'Self-branding, "micro-celebrity" and the rise of social media influencers', *Celebrity Studies*, 8(2): 191–208.

Kindynis, T. (2016) 'Urban exploration: from subterranea to spectacle', *British Journal of Criminology*, 57(4): 982–1001.

Kotzé, J. (2018) 'Criminology or zemiology? Yes, please! On the refusal of choice between false alternatives', in J. Kotzë and A. Boukli (eds) *Zemiology: Reconnecting Crime and Social Harm*, Basingstoke: Palgrave Macmillan, pp 85–106.

Kotzé, J., and Antonopoulos, G. (2019) 'Boosting bodily capital: maintaining masculinity aesthetic pleasure and instrumental utility through the consumption of steroids', *Journal of Consumer Culture*, 21(3): 683–700.

Kotzé, J., and Lloyd, A. (2022) *Making Sense of Ultra-realism: Contemporary Criminological Theory through the Lens of Popular Culture*, Bingley, UK: Emerald Publishing.

Kumar, K. (1988) 'From work to employment and unemployment', in R. Pahl (ed) *On Work: Historical, Comparative and Theoretical Perspectives*, Oxford: Blackwell, pp 138–64.

Lacan, J. (1997) *The Seminar of Jacques Lacan: Book III,* New York: W. W. Norton & Company.

Lacan, J. (2007) *Ecrits*, London: W. W. Norton & Company.

Large, J. (2018) 'Spot the fashion victim(s): the importance of rethinking harm within the context of fashion counterfeiting', in A. Boukli and J. Kotzé (eds) *Zemiology: Reconnecting Crime and Social Harm*, Basingstoke: Palgrave Macmillan, pp 223–44.

Large, J. (2019) *The Consumption of Counterfeit Fashion*, London: Palgrave Macmillan.

Lavorgna, A. (2014) 'The online trade in counterfeit pharmaceuticals: new criminal opportunities, trends and challenges', *European Journal of Criminology*, 12(2): 226–41.

Lazzarato, M. (2015) *Governing by Debt*, Los Angeles, CA: Semiotext(e).

Levy, H.S. (1966) *Chinese Footbinding: The History of a Curious Erotic Custom*, New York: W. Rawls, pp 37–63.

Liebow, E. (2003) *Tally's Corner: A Study of Negro Street Corner Men* (2nd edn), London: Rowman & Littlefield Publishers.

Lister, M., Dovey, J., Giddings, S., Grant, I., and Kelly, K. (2009) *New Media: A Critical Introduction* (2nd edn), London: Routledge.

Lloyd, A. (2012) 'Working to live, not living to work: work, leisure and youth identity among call centre workers in North East England', *Current Sociology*, 60(5): 619–35.

Lloyd, A. (2013) *Labour Markets and Identity on the Post-Industrial Assembly Line*, London: Routledge.

Lloyd, A. (2018) 'Serving up harm: systemic violence, transitions to adulthood and the service economy', in A. Boukli and J. Kotzé (eds) *Zemiology: Reconnecting Crime and Social Harm*, Basingstoke: Palgrave Macmillan, pp 245–64.

Lowe, P. (2006) 'Counterfeiting: links to organised crime and terrorist funding', *Journal of Financial Crime*, 13(2): 255–7.

MacCallum, F., and Widdows, H. (2018) 'Altered images: understanding the influence of unrealistic images and beauty aspirations', *Health Care Analysis*, 26: 235–45.

MacCarthy, B.L., Jayarathne, P.G.S.A. (2010) 'Fast fashion: achieving global quick response (GQR) in the internationally dispersed clothing industry', in T. Cheng and T.M. Choi (eds) *Innovative Quick Response Programs in Logistics and Supply Chain Management*, International Handbooks on Information Systems, Berlin and Heidelberg: Springer.

McCartney, S. (2005) *The Fake Factor: Why We Love Brands but Buy Fakes*, London: Cyan.

McGowan, T. (2016) *Capitalism and Desire: The Psychic Cost of Free Markets*, New York: Columbia University Press.

McKay, S. (2020) 'Knowing It could kill you isn't a deterrent': the deadly trade in diet pills', [online] 21 July 2020, *The Guardian*, Available from: https://www.theguardian.com/society/2020/jul/21/dnp-deadly-diet-pills-online-trade [Accessed 4 December 2020].

Mears, A. (2014) 'Aesthetic labor for the sociologies of work, gender and beauty', *Sociology Compass*, 8(12): 1330–43.

Mental Health Foundation (2021) 'Mental Health Foundation criticises Love Island', [online], 3 June 2019, Mental Health Foundation, Available from: https://www.mentalhealth.org.uk/about-us/news/mental-health-foundation-criticises-new-series-love-island-it-releases-new-statistics-about-body [Accessed 20 June 2020].

Meshi, D., Tamir, D., and Heekeren, H. (2015) 'The emerging neuroscience of social media', *Trends in Cognitive Sciences*, 19(12): 771–82.

Mestrovic, S. (2003) *Thorstein Veblen: On Culture and Society*, London: Sage Publications.

MHRA (2023) 'Ozempic (semaglutide) and Saxenda (liraglutide): vigilance required due to potentially harmful falsified products', [online] 23 November 2024, GOV.UK, Available from: https://www.gov.uk/drug-safety-update/ozempicv-semaglutide-and-saxenda-liraglutide-vigilance-required-due-to-potentially-harmful-falsified-products [Accessed 30 January 2024].

Monaghan., L.F. (2001) *Bodybuilding, Drugs and Risk*, London: Routledge.

Montoya, I., and Jano, E. (2007) 'Online pharmacies: safety and regulatory considerations', *International Journal of Health Services*, 37(2): 279–89.

Morgan, L.R., and Birtwistle, G. (2009) 'An investigation of young fashion consumers' disposal habits', *International Journal of Consumer Studies*, 33(2): 190–8.

Mulrooney, K., and van de Ven, K. (2019) 'The fittest on earth: performance and image enhancing drugs use within UK CrossFit communities', in T. Raymen and O. Smith (eds) *Deviant Leisure: Criminological Perspectives on Leisure and Harm,* London: Palgrave Macmillan, pp 161–86.

Naylor, R.T. (2002) *Wages of Crime: Black Markets, Illegal Finance, and the Underworld Economy,* London: Cornell University Press.

New York Times (1888) 'Choked by His collar', [online] 15 September 1888, Times Machine, Available from: https://timesmachine.nytimes.com/timesmachine/1888/09/15/106193425.pdf?pdf_redirect=true&ip=0 [Accessed 20 February 2024].

New York Times (1903) 'Corset steel in her heart', [online] 30 October 1903, Times Machine, Available from: https://timesmachine.nytimes.com/timesmachine/1903/10/30/105063971.pdf?pdf_redirect=true&ip=0 [Accessed 20 February 2024].

Nicholls, E. (2019) *Negotiating Femininities in the Neoliberal Night-Time Economy: Too Much of a Girl?,* London: Palgrave Macmillan.

Nowotny, H. (1994) *Time: The Modern and Postmodern Experience*, Cambridge: Polity Press.

Nuffield Council on Bioethics (2017) *Cosmetic Procedures: Ethical Issues*, [online] 22 June 2017, Nuffield Bioethics, Available from: https://www.nuffieldbioethics.org/publications/cosmetic-procedures [Accessed 22 January 2024].

OECD (1998) *The Economic Impact of Counterfeiting*, Paris: OECD.

OECD (2008) *The Economic Impact of Counterfeiting and Piracy*, Paris: OECD.

OECD (2022) *Dangerous Fakes: Trade in Counterfeit Goods that Pose Health, Safety and Environmental Risks*, Illicit Trade, [online] 17 May 2022, OECD, Available from: https://www.oecd-ilibrary.org/governance/dangerous-fakes_117e352b-en [Accessed 10 November 2023].

Offer, A. (2001) 'Body weight and self-control in the United States and Britain since the 1950s', *Social History of Medicine*, 14(1): 79–106.

Office for National Statistics (ONS) (2024) *Young People Not in Education, Employment or Training (NEET), UK*, [online], 22 February 2024, ONS Statistical Bulletin, Available from: https://www.ons.gov.uk/employmentandlabourmarket/peoplenotinwork/unemployment/bulletins/youngpeoplenotineducationemploymentortrainingneet/february2024 [Accessed 13 April 2024].

Ogden, J. (1992) *Fat Chance! The Myth of Dieting Explained*, London: Routledge.

Paoli, L., and Donati, A. (2014) *The Sports Doping Market: Understanding Supply and Demand, and the Challenges of their Control*, London: Springer.

Passini, S. (2013) 'A binge-consuming culture: the effect of consumerism on social interactions in Western societies', *Culture and Psychology*, 19(3): 369–90.

Pemberton, S. (2015) *Harmful Societies: Understanding Social Harm*, Bristol: Policy Press.

Pfaller, R. (2017) *Interpassivity: The Aesthetics of Delegated Enjoyment*, Edinburgh: Edinburgh University Press.

Pollock, S., Taylor, S., Oyerinde, O., Numohamed, S., Dlova, N., Sarkar, R., Galadari, H., Manela-Azulay, M., Chung, H.S., Handog, E., and Kourish, S. (2021) 'The dark side of skin lightening: an international collaboration and review of a public health issue affecting dermatology', *International Journal of Women's Dermatology*, 7(2): 158–64.

Presdee, M. (2001) *Cultural Criminology and the Carnival of Crime*, London: Routledge.

Quinn, K., and Papacharissi, Z. (2018) 'Our networked selves: personal connection and relational maintenance in social media use', in J. Burgess, A. Marwick and T. Poell (eds) *The Sage Handbook of Social Media*, London: Sage Publications, pp 353–71.

Rackham, A. (2024) 'Growing skincare use by children is dangerous, say dermatologists', [online] 27 January 2024, BBC, Available from: https://www.bbc.co.uk/news/health-67993618 [Accessed 29 January 2024].

Raustiala, K., and Sprigman, C. (2012) *The Knockoff Economy: How Imitation Sparks Innovation,* Oxford: Oxford University Press.

Rawlinson, K. (2018) 'Breast enlargement ads shown during Love Island banned by ASA', [online] 17 October 2018, Available from: https://www.theguardian.com/tv-and-radio/2018/oct/17/breast-enlargement-ads-shown-during-love-island-banned-by-asa [Accessed 13 February 2020].

Raymen, T. (2018) *Parkour, Deviance and Leisure in the Late-Capitalist City*, Bingley, UK: Emerald Publishing.

Raymen, T., and Smith, O. (2016) 'What's deviance got to do with it? Black Friday sales, violence and hyper-conformity', *British Journal of Criminology*, 56(2): 389–405.

Raymen, T., and Smith, O. (2017) 'Lifestyle gambling, indebtedness and anxiety: a deviant leisure perspective', *Journal of Consumer Culture*, 20(4): 381–99.

Raymen, T., and Smith, O. (2019) 'Introduction: why leisure?', in T. Raymen and O. Smith (eds) *Deviant Leisure: Criminological Perspectives on Leisure and Harm*, London: Palgrave Macmillan, pp 1–14.

Responsible Mica Initiative (2018) *Towards a Responsible Indian Mica Supply Chain*, [online], Responsible Mica Initiative, Available from: http://www.responsible-mica-initiative.com/ [Accessed 5 November 2020].

Rigby, R. (2019) 'When less is more: the beauty bloggers exposing the industry's wasteful secret', [online] 3 April 2019, *The Guardian*, Available from: https://www.theguardian.com/fashion/2019/apr/03/when-less-is-more-the-beauty-bloggers-exposing-the-industrys-wasteful-secret [Accessed 3 October 2021].

Ritschel, C. (2018) 'Black henna tattoo warning after woman's children were left "permanently scarred"', [online] 17 July 2018, *The Independent*, Available from: https://www.independent.co.uk/life-style/black-henna-dangers-risk-scarring-warning-tattoo-temporary-chemical-burn-a8451756.html [Accessed 17 December 2023].

Ritzer, G., and Jurgenson, N. (2010) 'Production, consumption, prosumption', *Journal of Consumer Culture*, 10(1): 13–36.

Roberton, J. (2017) 'Fake make-up: the toxic truth you need to know this Christmas', [online] 5 December 2017, ITV News, Available from: https://www.itv.com/news/2017-12-06/fake-makeup-the-toxic-truth-you-need-to-know-this-christmas [Accessed 4 October 2020].

Rojek, C. (2010) *The Labour of Leisure: The Culture of Free Time*, London: Sage Publications.

Rosenthal, E.C. (2005) *The Era of Choice: The Ability to Choose and Its Transformation of Contemporary Life*, London: MIT Press.

Rowser, A.L. (2020) *Ethical Beauty Products*, New York: Rosen Publishing.

Royal Society for Public Health (2017) *#StatusOfMind: Social Media and Young People's Mental Health and Wellbeing*, [online] May 2017, Royal Society for Public Health, Available from: https://www.rsph.org.uk/our-work/campaigns/status-of-mind.html [Accessed 16 August 2023].

Ruggiero, V., and South, N. (1995) *Eurodrugs*, London: UCL Press.

Russell-Mayhew, S. Estefan, A., Moules, N.J., Lefebvre, D., Morhun, J.M., et al (2022) 'The optics of weight: expert perspectives from the panopticon and synopticon', *Psychology and Health*, 39(6): 823–37.

Rutter, J., and Bryce, J. (2008) 'The consumption of counterfeit goods: "here be pirates?"', *Sociology*, 42(6): 1146–64.

Salinas, M. (2018) 'The unusual suspects: an educated, legitimately employed drug dealing network', *International Criminal Justice Review*, 28(3): 226–42.

Sanders, C., and Angus Vail, D. (2008) *Customizing the Body: The Art and Culture of Tattooing*, Philadelphia, PA: Temple University Press.

Save Face (2019) 'Revealed: lip fillers are being offered to children in the UK', [online], Save Face, Available from: https://www.saveface.co.uk/revealed-lip-fillers-are-being-offered-to-children-in-the-uk/ [Accessed 12 January 2021].

Sharp, G., and Gerrard, Y. (2022) 'The body image "problem" on social media: novel directions for the field', *Body Image*, 41: 267–71.

Shen, A., and Antonopoulos, G. (2017) 'No banquet can do without liquor: alcohol counterfeiting in the people's republic of China', *Trends in Organised Crime*, 20(3–4): 273–95.

Shepherd, D., Whitman, K., Button, M., and Wilson, J.M. (2023) 'The impact of deviant social media influencers and consumer characteristics on purchasing counterfeit goods', *Deviant Behavior*, 44(12): 1746–60.

Smit, N., Vicanova, J., and Pavel, S. (2009) 'The hunt for natural skin whitening agents', *International Journal of Molecular Sciences*', 10(12): 5326–49.

Smith, O. (2014) *Contemporary Adulthood and the Night-Time Economy*, Basingstoke: Palgrave Macmillan.

Smith, O., and Raymen, T. (2018) 'Deviant leisure: a criminological perspective', *Theoretical Criminology*, 22(1): 63–82.

SOMO (2016) *Beauty and a Beast: Child Labour in India for Sparkling Cars and Cosmetics*, [online] March 2016, Centre for Research on Multinational Corporations, Available from: https://www.somo.nl/wp-content/uploads/2016/05/Beauty-and-a-Beast.pdf [Accessed 5 January 2022].

Southwood, I. (2011) *Non-Stop Inertia*, Winchester, UK: Zero Books.

Standing, G. (2011) *The Precariat: The New Dangerous Class*, London: Bloomsbury.

Steele, V. (2001) *The Corset: A Cultural History*, New Haven, CT: Yale University Press.

Stiegler, B. (2013) *Uncontrollable Societies of Disaffected Individuals*, Cambridge: Polity Press.

Sugiura, L., Pope, C., and Webber, C. (2012) 'Buying unlicensed slimming drugs from the web: a virtual ethnography', WebSci '12, Proceedings of the 4th Annual ACM Web Science Conference, pp 284–7.

Tate, S.A. (2017) 'Skin: post-feminist bleaching culture and the political vulnerability of blackness', in A.S. Elias, R. Gill and C. Scharff (eds) *Aesthetic Labour: Rethinking Beauty Politics in Neoliberalism,* London: Palgrave Macmillan, pp 199–214.

Taylor, J.D. (2013) *Negative Capitalism: Cynicism in the Neoliberal Era*, Winchester, UK: Zero Books.

Thieme, T. (2021) '"Shit wages" and side hustles: ordinary working lives in Nairobi, London and Berlin', in W. Monteith, D.O. Vicol and P. Williams (eds) *Beyond the Wage: Ordinary Work in Diverse Economies*, Bristol: Bristol University Press, pp 23–44.

Tiggemann, M., and Anderberg, I. (2019) 'Social media is not real: the effect of "Instagram vs reality" images on women's social comparison and body image', *New Media & Society*, 22(12): 2183–99.

Tom, G., Garibaldi, B., Zeng, Y., and Pilcher, J. (1998) 'Consumer demand for counterfeit goods', *Psychology and Marketing*, 15(5): 405–21.

Treadwell, J. (2008) 'Call the (fashion) police: how fashion becomes criminalised', *Papers from the British Society Criminology Conference*, 8(1): 117–33. Available from: http://www.britsoccrim.org/volume8/8Treadwell08.pdf [Accessed 18 March 2023].

Treadwell, J. (2011) 'From the car boot to booting it up? eBay, online counterfeit crime and the transformation of the criminal marketplace', *Criminology & Criminal Justice,* 12(2): 175–91.

Treadwell, J., Briggs, D., Winlow, S., and Hall, S. (2013) 'Shopocalypse now: consumer culture and the English riots of 2011', *British Journal of Criminology,* 53(1): 1–17.

Tudor, K. (2019) 'Symbolic survival and harm: serious fraud and consumer capitalism's perversion of the causa sui project', *British Journal of Criminology*, 59(5): 1237–53.

Tzanetakis, M., Kamphausen, G., Werse, B., and Laufenberg, R. (2016) 'The transparency of paradox. building trust, resolving disputes and optimising logistics on conventional and online drug markets', *International Journal of Drug Policy,* 35: 58–68.

Underhill, P. (2008) *Why We Buy: The Science of Shopping*, New York: Simon & Schuster.

UNEP (United Nations Environment Programme) (2015) *Plastic in Cosmetics: Are We Polluting the Environment Through Our Personal Care?* [online] 31 May 2015, UNEP Report, Available from: https://www.unep.org/resources/report/plastic-cosmetics-are-we-polluting-environment-through-our-personal-care [Accessed 4 March 2020].

United Nations (2019) 'UN launches drive to highlight environmental cost of staying fashionable', [online] 25 March 2019, UN News, Available from: https://news.un.org/en/story/2019/03/1035161 [Accessed 4 March 2020].

van de Ven, K., and Mulrooney, K.J.D. (2017) 'Social suppliers: exploring the cultural contours of the performance and image enhancing drug (PIED) market among bodybuilders in the Netherlands and Belgium', *International Journal of Drug Policy*, 40: 6–15.

van Duyne, P.C. (2005) 'Crime and commercial activity: an introduction to two half brothers', in P.C. van Duyne, K. von Lampe, M. van Dijck and J.L. Newell (eds) *The Organised Crime Economy: Managing Crime Markets in Europe*, Nijmegen: Wolf Legal Publishers, pp 1–17.

Veblen, T. (2005) *The Theory of the Leisure Class*, New York: Sentry Press.

Waldron, H.A. (1983) 'Did the Mad Hatter have mercury poisoning?', *British Medical Journal*, 287(6409): 1961.

Walker, D., and Joubert, H.E. (2011) 'Attitudes of injecting male anabolic androgenic steroid users to media influence, health messages and gender constructs', *Drugs and Alcohol Today*, 11(2): 56–70.

Walsh, A., and Rai, R. (2023) 'Weight loss injection hype fuels online black market', [online] 15 November 2023, BBC, Available from: https://www.bbc.co.uk/news/health-67414203 [Accessed 20 May 2024].

Wernick, A. (1991) *Promotional Culture: Advertising, Ideology and Symbolic Expression*, London: Sage Publications.

Wheeler, C.K., Said, H., Prucz, R., Rodrich, R.J., and Mathes, D.W. (2011) 'Social Media in plastic surgery practices: emerging trends in North America', *Aesthetic Surgery Journal*, 31(4): 435–41.

White, R., and Heckneberg, D. (2014) *Green Criminology: An Introduction to the Study of Environmental Harm*, Abingdon: Routledge.

Wickham, S., Bentley, L., Rose, T., Whitehead, M., Taylor-Robinson, D., and Barr, B. (2020) 'Effects on mental health of a UK welfare reform, Universal Credit: a longitudinal controlled study', *Lancet Public Health*, 5(3): 157–64.

Widdows, H. (2018) *Perfect Me: Beauty as an Ethical Ideal,* Woodstock, NY: Princeton University Press.

Widdows, H. (2021) 'Structural injustice and the requirements of beauty', *Journal of Social Philosophy,* 52(2): 251–69.

Wilcox, K., Min Kim, H., and Sen, S. (2009) 'Why do consumers buy counterfeit luxury brands?', *Journal of Marketing Research*', 46(2): 247–59.

Winlow, S. (2019) 'What lies beneath? Some notes on ultra-realism, and the intellectual foundations of the "deviant leisure" perspective', in T. Raymen and O. Smith (eds) *Deviant Leisure: Criminological Perspectives on Leisure and Harm,* London: Palgrave Macmillan, pp 45–66.

Winlow, S., and Hall, S. (2006) *Violent Night: Urban Leisure and Contemporary Culture*, Oxford: Berg.

Winlow, S., and Hall, S. (2009) 'Living for the weekend: youth identities in North East England', *Ethnography*, 10(1): 91–113.

Winlow, S., and Hall, S. (2013) *Rethinking Social Exclusion: The End of the Social*, London: Sage Publications.

Winlow, S., and Hall, S. (2016) 'Realist criminology and its discontents', *International Journal for Crime, Justice and Social Democracy*, 5(3): 80–94.

Winlow, S., and Hall, S. (2019) 'Shock and awe: on progressive minimalism and retreatism, and the new ultra-realism', *Critical Criminology*, 27(1): 21–36.

Winlow, S., Hall, S., and Treadwell, J. (2017) *The Rise of the Right: English Nationalism and the Transformation of Working-Class Politics,* Bristol: Policy Press.

Wolf, N. (2002) *The Beauty Myth: How Images of Beauty Are Used Against Women,* New York: Harper Collins Publisher.

Wood, M.A. (2016) 'Antisocial media and algorithmic deviancy amplification: Analysing the ID of Facebook's technological unconscious', *Theoretical Criminology*, 21(2): 168–85.

Wood, R. (2024) 'From aesthetic labour to affective labour: feminine beauty and body work as self-care in UK "lockdown"', *Gender, Place & Culture*, 31(1): 82–101.

Wrap (2023) *Textiles 2024 – Annual Progress Report 2022/23*, [online] The Waste and Resources Action Programme, Available from: https://www.wrap.ngo/resources/report/textiles-2030-annual-progress-update-2022-23 [Accessed 28 May 2024].

Yar, M. (2008) 'The other global drugs crisis: assessing the scope, impacts and drivers of the trade in dangerous counterfeit pharmaceuticals', *International Journal of Social Inquiry*, 1(1): 151–66.

Yar, M. (2012) 'Crime, media and the will-to-representation', *Crime, Media and Culture*, 8(3): 245–60.

Yurchisin, J., and Johnson, K. (2010) *Fashion and the Consumer*, London: Berg.

Žižek, S. (1997) *The Abyss of Freedom*, Ann Arbor: University of Michigan Press.

Žižek, S. (2002) *Welcome to the Desert of the Real*, London: Verso.

Žižek, S. (2006) *The Parallax View*, Cambridge, MA: MIT Press.

Žižek, S. (2008) *Violence: Six Sideways Reflection*, London: Verso.

Žižek, S. (2014) 'The impasses of consumerism', in teNeus (ed) *Prix Pictet 05: Consumption*, London: teNeus.

Index

D

E

Y

Z